5th Workshop on Language Analysis for Social Media

(LASM 2014)

Held at the 14th Conference of the European Chapter of the Association for Computational Linguistics

Gothenburg, Sweden
26-30 April 2014

ISBN: 978-1-63266-408-2

Printed from e-media with permission by:

Curran Associates, Inc.
57 Morehouse Lane
Red Hook, NY 12571

proceedings.com

Some format issues inherent in the e-media version may also appear in this print version.

Printed by Curran Associates, Inc. (2014)

For permission requests, please contact the Association for Computational Linguistics
at the address below.

Association for Computational Linguistics
209 N. Eighth Street
Stroudsburg, Pennsylvania 18360

Phone: 1-570-476-8006
Fax: 1-570-476-0860

acl@aclweb.org

Additional copies of this publication are available from:

Curran Associates, Inc.
57 Morehouse Lane
Red Hook, NY 12571 USA
Phone: 845-758-0400
Fax: 845-758-2634
Email: curran@proceedings.com
Web: www.proceedings.com

Introduction

These proceedings contain the papers presented at the 5th Workshop on Language Analysis in Social Media (LASM 2014). The workshop is held in Gothenburg, Sweden, on April 26–30, 2014, and hosted in conjunction with the 14th Conference of the European Chapter of the Association for Computational Linguistics.

Over the past few years, online social networking sites (Facebook, Twitter, Youtube, Flickr, MySpace, LinkedIn, Metacafe, Vimeo, etc.) have revolutionized the way we communicate with individuals, groups and communities, and altered everyday practices. The unprecedented volume and variety of user-generated content as well as the user interaction network constitute new opportunities for understanding social behavior and building socially-intelligent systems.

This 5th workshop attracted several submissions from around the world. Each paper was assigned to four reviewers. For the final workshop program, and for inclusion in these proceedings, nine regular papers were selected. The workshop program features two keynote presentations: one by Kalina Bontcheva, Senior Researcher in the Natural Language Processing Group, Department of Computer Science, University of Sheffield, and one on Industrial perspectives presented by NLP Technologies, Montreal Canada, on social media monitoring and innovative tools.

One of the goals of LASM 2014 was to reflect a wide range of different research efforts and results of language analysis with implications for fields such as natural language processing, computational linguistics, sociolinguistics and psycholinguistics. We invited original and unpublished research papers on all topics related to the analysis of language on social media, including the following topics:

- What are people talking about on social media?
- How are they expressing themselves?
- Why do they scribe?
- Natural language processing techniques for social media analysis
- How do language and social network properties interact?
- Semantic Web / Ontologies / Domain models to aid in social data understanding
- Characterizing Participants via Linguistic Analysis
- Language, Social Media and Human Behavior

This workshop would not have been possible without the hard work of many people. We would like to thank all Program Committee members and external reviewers for their effort in providing high-quality reviews in a timely manner. We thank all the authors who submitted their papers, as well as the authors whose papers were selected, for their help with preparing the final copy. We are in debt to the EACL 2014 Workshop co-Chairs. We would also like to thank our industry partners for their support and for making LASM 2014 a successful workshop; NLP Technologies, Microsoft Research and IBM Almaden.

March 2014

Atefeh Farzindar, Diana Inkpen, Michael Gamon, and Meena Nagarajan

Organizing Committee:

Atefeh Farzindar (NLP Technologies Inc. and Universite de Montreal Canada)
Diana Inkpen (University of Ottawa, Canada)
Michael Gamon (Microsoft Research, USA)
Meena Nagarajan (IBM Research, USA)

Program Committee:

Colin Cherry (NRC Canada)
Cindy Chung (University of Texas)
Munmun De Choudhury (Microsoft Research)
Jacob Eisenstein (Georgia Institute of Technology)
Jennifer Foster (Dublin City University)
Kevin Hass (Microsoft)
Guy Lapalme (Universite de Montreal)
Saif Mohammad (NRC Canada)
Smaranda Muresan (Rutgers University)
Alexander Osherenko (Humboldt-Universität zu Berlin)
Patrick Pantel (Microsoft Research)
Alan Ritter (University of Washington)
Mathieu Roche (Universite de Montpellier)
Victoria Rubin (University of Western Ontario)
Hassan Sayyadi (University of Maryland)
Valerie Shalin (Wright State)
Mike Thelwall (University of Wolverhampton)
Alessandro Valitutti (University of Helsinki)
Julien Velcin (Universite de Lyon)
Wei Xu (University of Washington)

Table of Contents

Conference Program

(9.00 am) Introductions

(9.05 am) Industrial Key Note:
Atefeh Farzindar, NLP Technologies, Montreal Canada
Industrial perspectives on social media monitoring and innovative tools

(9.15 am) Invited Key Note:
Kalina Bontcheva, Department of Computer Science, University of Sheffield
Natural Language Processing for Social Media: Are We There Yet?
(see *workshop web page* for abstract)

(10.30 am) Coffee Break

(11.00 am)

Mining Lexical Variants from Microblogs: An Unsupervised Multilingual Approach
Alejandro Mosquera and Paloma Moreda Pozo

(11.30 am)

Estimating Time to Event from Tweets Using Temporal Expressions
Ali Hürriyetoğlu, Nelleke Oostdijk and Antal van den Bosch

(12.00 pm)

Accurate Language Identification of Twitter Messages
Marco Lui and Timothy Baldwin

(12.30 pm) Lunch Break

(2.00 pm)

The (Un)Predictability of Emotional Hashtags in Twitter
Florian Kunneman, Christine Liebrecht and Antal van den Bosch

(continued)

(2.30 pm)

Finding Arguing Expressions of Divergent Viewpoints in Online Debates
Amine Trabelsi and Osmar R. Zaiane

(3.00 pm)

Aspect Term Extraction for Sentiment Analysis: New Datasets, New Evaluation Measures and an Improved Unsupervised Method
John Pavlopoulos and Ion Androutsopoulos

(3.30 pm) Coffee Break

(4.00 pm)

Vowel and Diacritic Restoration for Social Media Texts
Kübra Adali and Gülşen Eryiğit

(4.30 pm)

A Cascaded Approach for Social Media Text Normalization of Turkish
Dilara Torunoğlu and Gülşen Eryiğit

(5.00 pm)

Experiments to Improve Named Entity Recognition on Turkish Tweets
Dilek Kucuk and Ralf Steinberger

(5.30 pm) Closing Remarks

Mining Lexical Variants from Microblogs: An Unsupervised Multilingual Approach

Alejandro Mosquera
University of Alicante
San Vicente del Raspeig s/n - 03690
Alicante, Spain
amosquera@dlsi.ua.es

Paloma Moreda
University of Alicante
San Vicente del Raspeig s/n - 03690
Alicante, Spain
moreda@dlsi.ua.es

Abstract

User-generated content has become a recurrent resource for NLP tools and applications, hence many efforts have been made lately in order to handle the noise present in short social media texts. The use of normalisation techniques has been proven useful for identifying and replacing lexical variants on some of the most informal genres such as microblogs. But annotated data is needed in order to train and evaluate these systems, which usually involves a costly process. Until now, most of these approaches have been focused on English and they were not taking into account demographic variables such as the user location and gender. In this paper we describe the methodology used for automatically mining a corpus of variant and normalisation pairs from English and Spanish tweets.

1 Introduction

User-generated content (UGC), and specially the microblog genre, has become an interesting resource for Natural Language Processing (NLP) tools and applications. Many are the advantages of exploiting this real-time stream of multilingual textual data. Popular applications such as Twitter has an heterogeneous user base of almost 600 million users that generate more than 60 million new tweets every day. For this reason, Twitter has become one of the most used sources of textual data for NLP with several applications such as sentiment analysis (Tumasjan et al., 2010) or realtime event detection (Sakaki et al., 2010). Recent advances on machine translation or information retrieval systems have been also making an extensive use of UGC for both training and evaluation purposes. However, tweets can be very noisy and sometimes hard to understand for both humans (Mosquera et al., 2012) and NLP applications (Wang and Ng, 2013), so an additional preprocessing step is usually required.

There have been different perceptions regarding the lexical quality of social media (Rello and Baeza-Yates, 2012) (Baldwin et al., 2013) and even others suggested that 40% of the messages of Twitter were "pointless babble" (PearAnalytics, 2009). Most of the out of vocabulary (OOV) words present in social media texts can be catalogued as lexical variants (e.g. "See u 2moro" $\rightarrow$ "See you tomorrow"), that are words lexically related with their canonic form.

The use of text normalisation techniques has been proven useful in order to clean short and informal texts such as tweets. However, the evaluation of these systems requires annotated data, which usually involves costly human annotations. There are previous works about automatically constructing normalisation dictionaries, but until now, most of these approaches have been focused on English and they were not taking into account demographic variants. In this paper we describe the methodology used for automatically mining lexical variants from English and Spanish tweets associated to a set of headwords. These formal and informal pairs can be later used to train and evaluate existing social media text normalisation systems. Additional metadata from Twitter such as geographic location and user gender is also collected, opening the possibility to model and analyse gender or location-specific variants.

This paper is organised as follows. We describe the related work in Section 2. We then describe our variant mining methodology in Section 3. The obtained results are presented in Section 4. Section 5, draws the conclusions and future work.

2 Related Work

One way to handle the performance drop of NLP tools on user-generated content (Foster et al., 2011) is to re-train existing models on these informal genres (Gimpel et al., 2011), (Liu et al., 2011b). Another approaches make use of preprocessing techniques such as text normalisation in order to minimise the social media textual noise (Han et al., 2013), (Mosquera and Moreda, 2012) where OOV words were first identified and then substituted using lexical and phonetic edit distances. In order to enhance both precision and recall both OOV detection and translation dictionaries were used. Moreover, the creative nature of informal writing and the low availability of manually-annotated corpora can make the improvement and evaluation of these systems challenging.

Motivated by the lack of annotated data and the large amount of OOV words contained in Twitter, several approaches for automatically constructing a lexical normalisation dictionary were proposed; In (Gouws et al., 2011) a normalisation lexicon is generated based on distributional and string similarity (Lodhi et al., 2002) from Twitter. Using a similar technique, a wider-coverage dictionary is constructed in (Han et al., 2012) based on contextually-similar (OOV, IV) pairs. More recently, (Hassan and Menezes, 2013) introduced another context-based approach using random walks on a contextual similarity graph.

Distributional-based methods can have some drawbacks: they rely heavily on pairwise comparisons that make them computationally expensive, and as the normalisation candidates are selected based on context similarity they can be sensitive to domain-specific variants that share similar contexts. Moreover, these approaches were focusing on extracting English lexical variants from social media texts, but due the heterogeneity of its users, lexical distributions can be influenced by geographical factors (Eisenstein et al., 2010) or even gender (Thomson and Murachver, 2001).

To the best of our knowledge, there are not multilingual approaches for mining lexical variants from short, noisy texts that also take into account demographic variables. For this reason, we present an unsupervised method for mining English and Spanish lexical variants from Twitter that collects demographic and contextual information. These obtained pairs can be later used for training and evaluating text normalisation and inverse text normalisation systems.

3 Lexical Variant Mining

Lexical variants are typically formed from their standard forms through regular processes (Thurlow and Brown, 2003) and these can be modelled by using a set of basic character transformation rules such as letter insertion, deletion or substitution (Liu et al., 2011a) e.g. ("tmrrw" → "2morrow") and combination of these ("2moro"). The relation between formal and informal pairs is not always 1-to-1, two different formal words can share the same lexical variant ("t" in Spanish can represent "te" or "tú") and one formal word can have many different variants (e.g. "see you" us commonly shortened as "c ya" or "see u"). As a difference with previous approaches based on contextual and distributional similarity, we have chosen to model the generation of variant candidates from a set of headwords using transformation rules. These candidates are later validated based on their presence on a popular microblog service, used in this case as a high-coverage corpus.

3.1 Candidate Generation

We have defined a set of 6 basic transformation rules (see Table 1) in order to automatically generate candidate lexical variants from the 300k most frequent words of Web 1T 5-gram (English) (Brants and Franz, 2006) and SUBTLEX-SP (Spanish) (Cuetos et al., 2011) corpora.

Rule	Example
a) Character duplication	"goal" → "gooal"
b) Number transliteration	"cansados" → "cansa2"
c) Character deletion	"tomorrow" → "tomrrw"
d) Character replacement	"friend" → "freend"
e) Character transposition	"maybe" → "mabye"
f) Phonetic substitution	"coche" → "coxe"
g) Combination of above	"coche" → "coxeee"

Table 1: Transformation rules.

As modelling some variants may need more than one basic operation, and lexically-related variants are usually in an edit distance t where $t <= 3$ (Han et al., 2013), the aforementioned rules were implemented using an engine based on stacked transducers with the possibility to apply a maximum of three concurrent transformations:

(a) Character duplication: For words with n characters, while n>19 each character were duplicated n times (∀ n>0, n<4), generating n^3 candidate variants.

(b) Number transliteration: Words and numbers are transliterated following the language rules defined in Table 2.

Rule	Lang.
"uno" → "1"	SP
"dos" → "2"	SP
"one" → "1"	EN
"two" → "2"	EN
"to" → "2"	EN
"three" → "3"	EN
"for" → "4"	EN
"four" → "4"	EN
"eight" → "8"	EN
"be" → "b"	EN
"a" → "4"	EN
"e" → "3"	EN
"o" → "0"	EN
"s" → "5"	EN
"g" → "6"	EN
"t" → "7"	EN
"l" → "1"	EN

Table 2: Transliteration table for English and Spanish.

(c) Character deletion: The candidate variants from all possible one character deletion combinations plus the consonant skeleton of the word will be generated.

(d) Character replacement: Candidate variants are generated by replacing n characters (∀ n>0, n<7) by their neighbours taking into account a QWERTY keyboard and an edit distance of 1.

(e) Character transposition: In order to generate candidate lexical variants the position of adjacent characters are exchanged.

(f) Phonetic substitution: A maximum of three character n-grams are substituted for characters that sound similar following different rules for Spanish (Table 3) and English (Table 4).

3.2 Candidate Selection

We have explored several approaches for filtering common typographical errors and misspellings, as these are unintentional and can not be technically considered lexical variants, in order to do this we have used supervised machine learning techniques. Also, with aim to filter uncommon or low quality variants, the Rovereto Twitter corpus (Herdagdelen, 2013) was initially used in order to rank the English candidates present in the corpus by their frequencies. The 38% of the variants generated by one transformation were successfully found, however, performing direct Twitter search API queries resulted to have better coverage than using a static corpus (90% for English variants).

Rule
"b"→["v" or "w"]
"c"→["k"]
"s"→["z"]
"z"→["s"]
"c"→["s"]
"x"→["s"]
"ñ"→["ni"]
"ch"→["x"]
"gu"→["w"]
"qu"→["k"]
"ll"→["y"]
"ge"→["je"]
"gi"→["ji"]
"ll"→["i"]
"hue"→["we"]

Table 3: Phonetic substitution table for Spanish.

3.2.1 Intentionality Filtering

Given an OOV word *a* and its IV version *b* we have extracted character transformation rules from *a* to *b* using the longest common substring (LCS) algorithm (See Table 5). These lists of transformations were encoded as a numeric array where the number each transformation counts were stored. We have used NLTK (Bird, 2006) and the SequenceMatcher Python class in order to extract those sets of transformations taking into account also the position of the character (beginning, middle or at the end of the word).

A two-class SVM (Vapnik, 1995) model has ben trained using a linear kernel with a corpus composed by 4200 formal-variant pairs extracted from Twitter [1], SMS[2] and a corpus of the 4200 most common misspellings [3]. In table 6 we show the k-fold cross-validation results (k=10) of the model, obtaining a 87% F1. This model has been used in order to filter the English candidate variants classified as not-intentional.

To the best of our knowledge there are not similar annotated resources for Spanish, so this classifier was developed only for English variants. However, would be possible to adapt it to work for

[1] *http : //ww2.cs.mu.oz.au/ hanb/emnlp.tgz*
[2] *http : //www.cel.iitkgp.ernet.in/ monojit/sms*
[3] *http : //aspell.net/test/common − all/*

Rule
"i"→["e"]
"o"→["a"]
"u"→["o"]
"s"→["z"]
"f"→["ph"]
"j"→["ge" or "g"]
"n"→["kn" or "gn"]
"r"→["wr"]
"z"→["se" or "s"]
"ea"→["e"]
"ex"→["x"]
"ae"→["ay" or "ai" or "a"]
"ee"→["ea" or "ie" or "e"]
"ie"→["igh" or "y" or "i"]
"oe"→["oa" or "ow" or "o"]
"oo"→["ou" or "u"]
"ar"→["a"]
"ur"→["ir" or "er" or "ear" or "or"]
"or"→["oor" or "ar"]
"au"→["aw" or "a"]
"er"→["e"]
"ow"→["ou"]
"oi"→["oy"]
"sh"→["ss" or "ch"]
"ex"→["x"]
"sh"→["ss" or "ch"]
"ng"→["n"]
"air"→["ear" or "are"]
"ear"→["eer" or "ere"]

Table 4: Phonetic substitution table for English.

another languages if the adequate corpora is provided. Because of the lack of this intentionality detection step, the number of generated candidate variants for Spanish was filtered by taking into account the number of transformations, removing all the variants generated by more than two operations.

3.2.2 Twitter Search

The variants filtered during the previous step were searched on the real time Twitter stream for a period of two months by processing more than 7.5 million tweets. Their absolute frequencies n were used as a weighting factor in order to discard not used words ($n > 0$). Additionally, variants present in another languages rather than English or Spanish were ignored by using the language identification tags present in Twitter metadata.

There were important differences between the final number of selected candidates for Spanish, with 6 times less variant pairs and English (see Table 7). Spanish language uses diacritics that are commonly ignored on informal writing, for this reason there is a higher number of possible combinations for candidate words that would not generate valid or used lexical variants.

Formal/Informal pair	Transf.	Pos.
house → h0use	o → 0	middle
campaign → campaing	n → ∅	end
	∅ → n	middle
happy → :)	happy → :)	middle
embarrass → embarass	r→ ∅	middle
acquaintance →	∅ → q	middle
aqcuaintance	q → ∅	middle
virtually → virtualy	l→ ∅	middle
cats → catz	s→ z	end

Table 5: Example of formal/informal pairs and the extract transformations.

Method	Precision	Recall	F1
SVM	0.831	0.824	0.827
SVM+Pos.	0.878	0.874	0.876

Formal/Informal pair	Verdict
you → yu	intentional
accommodate → acommodate	unintentional
business → bussiness	unintentional
doing → doin	intentional
acquaintance → aqcuaintance	unintentional
basically → basicly	unintentional
rules → rulez	intentional

Table 6: Cross-validation results of intentionality classification with examples.

4 Results

Besides the original message and the context of the searched variant, additional metadata has been collected from each tweet such as the gender and the location of the user. In Twitter the gender is not explicitly available, for this reason we applied an heuristic approach based on the first name as it is reported in the user profile. In order to do this, two list of male and female names were used: the 1990 US census data [4] and popular baby names from the US Social Security Administration's statistics between 1960 and 2010 [5].

We have analysed the gender and language distribution of the 6 transformation rules across the mined pairs (see Figure 1). On the one hand, lexical variants generated by duplicating characters were the most popular specially between female

[4] $census.gov/genealogy/www/data/1990surnames$
[5] $ssa.gov/cgi - bin/popularnames.cgi$

Candidates	Selected	Lang.
2456627	48550	EN
1374078	8647	SP

Table 7: Number of generated and selected variants after Twitter search.

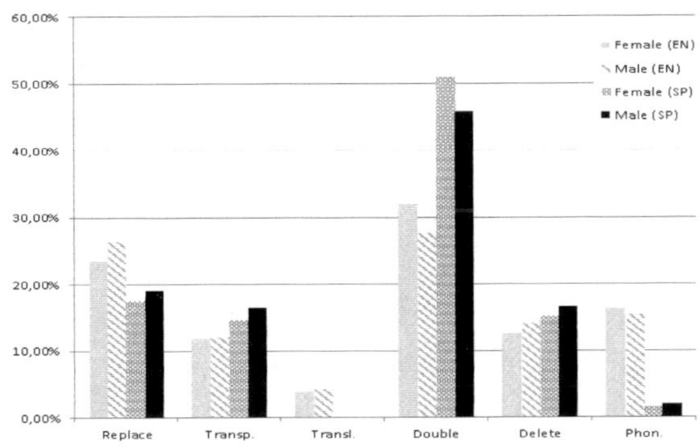

Figure 1: Transformation trends by gender.

users with a 5% more than their male counterparts. On the other hand, variants generated by character replacement and deletion were found a 2% more on tweets from male users. The differences between English and Spanish were notable, mostly regarding the use of transliterations, that were not found on Spanish tweets, and phonetic substitutions, ten times less frequent than in English tweets.

For the distribution of transformations across geographic areas, we have just taken into account the countries where the analysed languages have an official status. Lexical variants found in Tweets from another areas are grouped into the "Non-official" label (see Figure 2). The biggest differences were found on the use of transliterations (higher in UK and Ireland with more than a 5%) and phonetic substitutions (higher in Pakistani users with more than a 22%). Transformation frequencies from non-official English speaking countries were very similar as the ones registered for users based on United States and Canada.

Spanish results were less uniform and showed more variance respect the use of character duplication (57% in Argentina), character replacement (more than 24% in Mexico and Guatemala) and character transposition (with more than a 19% for users from Cuba, Colombia and Mexico) (see Figure 3).

5 Conclusions and Future Work

In this paper we have described a multilingual and unsupervised method for mining English and Spanish lexical variants from Twitter with aim to close the gap regarding the lack of annotated corpora. These obtained pairs can be later used for the training and evaluation of text normalisation systems without the need of costly human annotations. Furthermore, the gathered demographic and contextual information can be used in order to model and generate variants similar to those that can be found on specific geographic areas. This has interesting applications in the field of inverse text normalisation, that are left to a future work. We also intend to explore the benefits of feature engineering for the detection and categorisation of lexical variants using machine learning techniques.

Acknowledgments

This research is partially funded by the European Commission under the Seventh (FP7 - 2007- 2013) Framework Programme for Research and Technological Development through the FIRST project (FP7-287607). This publication reflects the views only of the author, and the Commission cannot be held responsible for any use which may be made of the information contained therein. Moreover, it has been partially funded by the Spanish Government through the project "Análisis de Tendencias Mediante Técnicas de Opinión Semántica" (TIN2012-38536-C03-03) and "Técnicas de Deconstrucción en la Tecnologías del Lenguaje Humano" (TIN2012-31224).

References

Timothy Baldwin, Paul Cook, Marco Lui, Andrew MacKinlay, and Li Wang. 2013. How noisy social media text, how diffrnt social media sources. In *Proceedings of the Sixth International Joint Conference on Natural Language Processing*, pages 356–364.

Steven Bird. 2006. Nltk: the natural language toolkit. In *Proceedings of the COLING/ACL on Interactive presentation sessions*, COLING-ACL '06, pages 69–72, Stroudsburg, PA, USA. Association for Computational Linguistics.

Thorsten Brants and Alex Franz. 2006. Web 1T 5-gram corpus version 1. Technical report, Google Research.

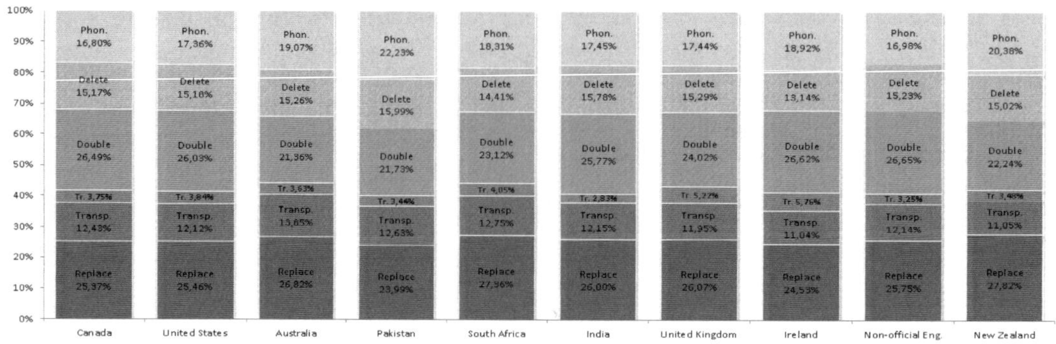

Figure 2: Transformation trends by English-speaking countries.

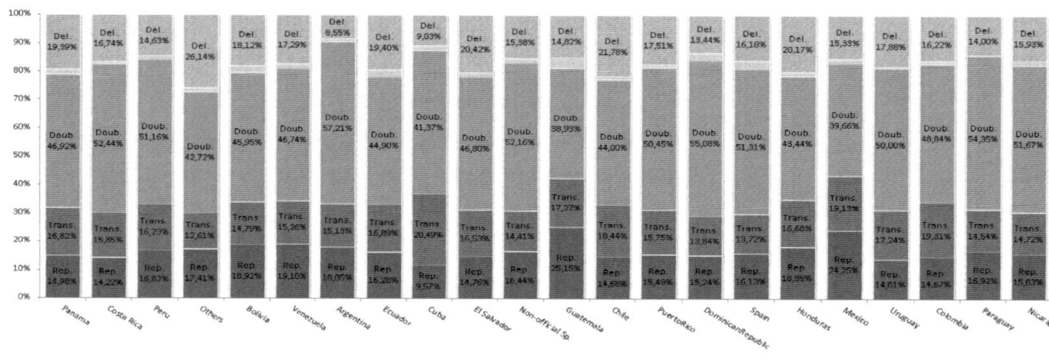

Figure 3: Transformation trends by Spanish-speaking countries.

Fernando Cuetos, Maria Glez-Nosti, Anala Barbn, and Marc Brysbaert. 2011. Subtlex-esp: Spanish word frequencies based on film subtitles. *Psicolgica*, 32(2).

Jacob Eisenstein, Brendan O'Connor, Noah A. Smith, and Eric P. Xing. 2010. A latent variable model for geographic lexical variation. In *Proceedings of the 2010 Conference on Empirical Methods in Natural Language Processing*, EMNLP '10, pages 1277–1287, Stroudsburg, PA, USA. Association for Computational Linguistics.

Jennifer Foster, Özlem Çetinoglu, Joachim Wagner, Joseph Le Roux, Stephen Hogan, Joakim Nivre, Deirdre Hogan, and Josef van Genabith. 2011. #hardtoparse: Pos tagging and parsing the twitterverse. In *Analyzing Microtext*, volume WS-11-05 of *AAAI Workshops*. AAAI.

Kevin Gimpel, Nathan Schneider, Brendan O'Connor, Dipanjan Das, Daniel Mills, Jacob Eisenstein, Michael Heilman, Dani Yogatama, Jeffrey Flanigan, and Noah A. Smith. 2011. Part-of-speech tagging for twitter: annotation, features, and experiments. In *Proceedings of the 49th Annual Meeting of the Association for Computational Linguistics: Human Language Technologies: short papers - Volume 2*, HLT '11, pages 42–47, Stroudsburg, PA, USA. Association for Computational Linguistics.

S. Gouws, D. Hovy, and D. Metzler. 2011. Unsupervised mining of lexical variants from noisy text. In *Proceedings of the First workshop on Unsupervised Learning in NLP*, page 82–90.

Bo Han, Paul Cook, and Timothy Baldwin. 2012. Automatically constructing a normalisation dictionary for microblogs. In *Proceedings of the 2012 Joint Conference on Empirical Methods in Natural Language Processing and Computational Natural Language Learning (EMNLP-CoNLL 2012)*, pages 421–432, Jeju Island, Korea.

Bo Han, Paul Cook, and Timothy Baldwin. 2013. Lexical normalization for social media text. *ACM Trans. Intell. Syst. Technol.*, 4(1):5:1–5:27, February.

Hany Hassan and Arul Menezes. 2013. Social text normalization using contextual graph random walks. In *Proceedings of the 51st Annual Meeting of the Association for Computational Linguistics (Volume 1: Long Papers)*, pages 1577–1586, Sofia, Bulgaria, August. Association for Computational Linguistics.

Ama Herdagdelen. 2013. Twitter n-gram corpus with demographic metadata. *Language Resources and Evaluation*, 47(4):1127–1147.

Fei Liu, Fuliang Weng, Bingqing Wang, and Yang Liu. 2011a. Insertion, deletion, or substitution?: Normalizing text messages without pre-categorization nor supervision. In *Proceedings of the 49th Annual Meeting of the Association for Computational Linguistics: Human Language Technologies: Short Papers - Volume 2*, HLT '11, pages 71–76, Stroudsburg, PA, USA. Association for Computational Linguistics.

Xiaohua Liu, Shaodian Zhang, Furu Wei, and Ming Zhou. 2011b. Recognizing named entities in tweets. In *Proceedings of the 49th Annual Meeting of the Association for Computational Linguistics: Human Language Technologies - Volume 1*, HLT '11, pages 359–367, Stroudsburg, PA, USA. Association for Computational Linguistics.

Huma Lodhi, Craig Saunders, John Shawe-Taylor, Nello Cristianini, and Chris Watkins. 2002. Text classification using string kernels. *J. Mach. Learn. Res.*, 2:419–444, March.

Alejandro Mosquera and Paloma Moreda. 2012. Tenor: A lexical normalisation tool for spanish web 2.0 texts. In *Text, Speech and Dialogue - 15th International Conference (TSD 2012)*. Springer.

Alejandro Mosquera, Elena Lloret, and Paloma Moreda. 2012. Towards facilitating the accessibility of web 2.0 texts through text normalisation. In *Proceedings of the LREC workshop: Natural Language Processing for Improving Textual Accessibility (NLP4ITA) ; Istanbul, Turkey.*, pages 9–14.

PearAnalytics. 2009. Twitter study. In *Retrieved December 15, 2009 from http://pearanalytics.com/wp-content/uploads/2009/08/Twitter-Study-August-2009.pdf.*

Luz Rello and Ricardo A Baeza-Yates. 2012. Social media is not that bad! the lexical quality of social media. In *ICWSM*.

Takeshi Sakaki, Makoto Okazaki, and Yutaka Matsuo. 2010. Earthquake shakes twitter users: Real-time event detection by social sensors. In *Proceedings of the 19th International Conference on World Wide Web*, WWW '10, pages 851–860, New York, NY, USA. ACM.

Robert Thomson and Tamar Murachver. 2001. Predicting gender from electronic discourse.

Thurlow and Brown. 2003. Generation txt? the sociolinguistics of young people's text-messaging.

A. Tumasjan, T.O. Sprenger, P.G. Sandner, and I.M. Welpe. 2010. Predicting elections with twitter: What 140 characters reveal about political sentiment. In *Proceedings of the Fourth International AAAI Conference on Weblogs and Social Media*, pages 178–185.

Vladimir N. Vapnik. 1995. *The nature of statistical learning theory*. Springer-Verlag New York, Inc., New York, NY, USA.

Pidong Wang and Hwee Tou Ng. 2013. A beam-search decoder for normalization of social media text with application to machine translation. In *HLT-NAACL*, pages 471–481.

Estimating Time to Event from Tweets Using Temporal Expressions

Ali Hürriyetoğlu, Nelleke Oostdijk, and Antal van den Bosch
Centre for Language Studies
Radboud University Nijmegen
P.O. Box 9103, NL-6500 HD Nijmegen, The Netherlands
{a.hurriyetoglu,n.oostdijk,a.vandenbosch}@let.ru.nl

Abstract

Given a stream of Twitter messages about an event, we investigate the predictive power of temporal expressions in the messages to estimate the time to event (TTE). From labeled training data we learn average TTE estimates of temporal expressions and combinations thereof, and define basic rules to compute the time to event from temporal expressions, so that when they occur in a tweet that mentions an event we can generate a prediction. We show in a case study on soccer matches that our estimations are off by about eight hours on average in terms of mean absolute error.

1 Introduction

Textual information streams such as those produced by news media and by social media reflect what is happening in the real world. These streams often contain explicit pointers to future events that may interest or concern a potentially large amount of people. Besides media-specific markers such as event-specific hashtags in messages on Twitter[1], these messages may contain explicit markers of place and time that help the receivers of the message disambiguate and pinpoint the event on the map and calendar.

The automated analysis of streaming text messages can play a role in catching these important events. Part of this analysis may be the identification of the future start time of the event, so that the event can be placed on the calendar and appropriate action may be taken by the receiver of the message, such as ordering tickets, planning a security operation, or starting a journalistic investigation. The automated identification of the time to event (TTE) should be as accurate and come early as possible. In this paper we explore a hybrid rule-based and data-driven method that exploits the explicit mentioning of temporal expressions to arrive at accurate and early TTE estimations.

The idea of publishing future calendars with potentially interesting events gathered (semi-) automatically for subscribers, possibly with personalization features and the option to harvest both social media and the general news, has been implemented already and is available through services such as Zapaday[2], Daybees[3], and Songkick[4]. To our knowledge, based on the public interfaces of these platforms, these services perform directed crawls of (structured) information sources, and identify exact date and time references in posts on these sources. They also manually curate event information, or collect this through crowdsourcing.

In this study we do not use a rule-based temporal tagger such as the HeidelTime tagger (Strötgen and Gertz, 2013), which searches for only a limited set of temporal expressions. Instead, we propose an approach that uses a large set of temporal expressions, created by using seed terms and generative rules, and a training method that automatically determines the TTE estimate to be associated with each temporal expression sequence in a data-driven way. Typically, rule-based systems do not use the implicit information provided by adverbs ('more' in 'three more days') and relations between non-subsequent elements, while machine-learning-based systems do not make use of the temporal logic inherent to temporal expressions; they may identify 'three more days' as a temporal expression but they lack the logical apparatus to compute that this implies a TTE of about 3×24 hours. To make use of the best of both worlds we propose a hybrid system which uses information about the distribution of temporal expressions

[1] http://twitter.com

[2] http://www.zapaday.com

[3] http://daybees.com/

[4] https://www.songkick.com/

as they are used in forward-looking social media messages in a training set of known events, and combines this estimation method with an extensive set of regular expressions that capture a large space of possible Dutch temporal expressions.

Thus, our proposed system analyzes social media text to find information about future events, and estimates how long it will take before the event takes place. The service offered by this system will be useful only if it generates accurate estimations of the time to event. Preferably, these accurate predictions should come as early as possible. Moreover, the system should be able, in the long run, to freely detect relevant future events that are not yet on any schedule we know in any language represented on social media. For now, in this paper we focus on estimating the starting time of scheduled events, and use past and known events for a controlled experiment involving Dutch twitter messages.

For our experiment we collected tweets referring to scheduled Dutch premier league soccer matches. This type of event generally triggers many anticipatory discussions on social media containing many temporal expressions. Given a held-out soccer match not used during training, our system predicts the time to the event based on individual tweets captured in a range from eight days before the event to the event time itself. Each estimation is based on the temporal expressions which occur in a particular twitter message. The mean absolute error of the predictions for each of the 60 soccer matches in our data set is off by about eight hours. The results are generated in a leave-one-out cross-validation setup[5].

This paper starts with describing the relation of our work to earlier research in Section 2. Section 3 describes the overall experimental setup, including a description of the data, the temporal expressions that were used, our two baselines, and the evaluation method used. Next, in Section 4 the results are presented. The results are analyzed and discussed in Section 5. We conclude with a summary of our main findings and make suggestions for the direction future research may take (Section 6).

[5]Tweet ID's, per tweet estimations, occurred time expressions and rules can be found at `http://www.ru.nl/lst/resources/`

2 Related Work

Future-reference analysis in textual data has been studied from different angles. In the realm of information retrieval the task is more commonly defined as seeking future temporal references in large document collections such as the Web by means of time queries (Baeza Yates, 2005). Various studies have used temporal expression elements as features in an automatic setting to improve the relevance estimation of a web document (Dias et al., 2011; Jatowt and Au Yeung, 2011). Information relevant to event times has been the focus of studies such as those by Becker *et al.* (2012) and Kawai et al. (2010).

Our research is aimed at estimating the time to event of an upcoming event as precisely as possible. Radinsky et al. (2012) approach this problem by learning from causality pairs in texts from long-ranging news articles. Noro et al. (2006) describe a machine-learning-based system for the identification of the time period in which an event will happen, such as in the morning or at night.

Some case studies are focused on detecting events as early as possible as their unfolding is fast. The study by Sakaki et al. (2010) describes a system which analyzes the flow of tweets in time and place mentioning an earthquake, to predict the unfolding quake pattern which may in turn provide just-in-time alerts to people residing in the locations that are likely to be struck shortly. Zielinski et al. (2012) developed an early warning system to detect natural disasters in a multilingual fashion and thereby support crisis management. The quick throughput of news in the Twitter network is the catalyst in these studies focusing on natural disasters. In our study, we rather rely on the slower build-up of clues in messages in days before an event, at a granularity level of hours.

Ritter et al. (2012) aim to create a calendar of events based on explicit date mentions and words typical of the event. They train on annotated open domain event mentions and use a rule-based temporal tagger. We aim to offer a more generic solution that makes use of a wider range of temporal expressions, including indirect and implicit expressions.

Weerkamp and De Rijke (2012) study this type of more generic patterns of anticipation in tweets, but focus on personal future activities, while we aim to predict as early as possible the time to event of events that affect and interest many users.

Our estimations do not target time periods such as mornings or evenings but on the number of hours remaining to the event.

TTE estimation of soccer matches has been the topic of several studies. Kunneman and Van den Bosch (2012) show that machine learning methods can differentiate between tweets posted before, during, and after a soccer match. Estimating the time to event of future matches from tweet streams has been studied by Hürriyetoglu et al. (2013), using local regression over word time series. In a related study, Tops et al. (2013) use support vector machines to classify the time to event in automatically discretized categories. At best these studies are about a day off in their predictions. Both studies investigate the use of temporal expressions, but fail to leverage the utility of this information source, most likely because they use limited sets of less than 20 regular expressions. In this study we scale up the number of temporal expressions.

3 Experimental Set-Up

We carried out a controlled case study in which we focused on Dutch premier league soccer matches as a type of scheduled event. These types of games have the advantage that they occur frequently, have a distinctive hashtag by convention, and often generate thousands to several tens of thousands of tweets per match.

Below we first describe the collection and composition of our data sets (Subsection 3.1) and the temporal expressions which were used to base our predictions upon (Subsection 3.2). Then, in Subsection 3.3, we describe our baselines and evaluation method.

3.1 Data Sets

We harvested tweets from twiqs.nl[6], a database of Dutch tweets collected from December 2010 onwards. We selected the six best performing teams of the Dutch premier league in 2011 and 2012[7], and queried all matches in which these teams played against each other in the calendar years 2011 and 2012. The collection procedure resulted in 269,999 tweets referring to 60 individual matches. The number of tweets per event ranges from 321 to 35,464, with a median of 2,723 tweets. Afterwards, we restricted the data to tweets sent within eight days before the match[8] and eliminated all retweets. This reduced the number of tweets in our final data set to 138,141 tweets.

In this experiment we are working on the assumption that the presence of a hashtag can be used as proxy for the topic addressed in a tweet. Inspecting a sample of tweets referring to recent soccer games not part of our data set, we developed the hypothesis that the position of the hashtag may have an effect as regards the topicality of the tweet. Hashtags that occur in final position (i.e. they are tweet-final or are only followed by one or more other hashtags) are typically metatags and therefore possibly more reliable as topic identifiers than tweet non-final hashtags which behave more like common content words in context. In order to be able to investigate the possible effect that the position of the hashtag might have, we split our data in the following two subsets:

FIN – comprising tweets in which the hashtag occurs in final position (as defined above); 84,533 tweets.

NFI – comprising tweets in which the hashtag occurs in non-final position; 53,608 tweets.

Each tweet in our data set has a time stamp of the moment (in seconds) it was posted. Moreover, for each soccer match we know exactly when it took place. This information is used to calculate for each tweet the actual time that remains to the start of the event and the absolute error in estimating the time to event.

3.2 Temporal Expressions

In the context of this paper temporal expressions are considered to be words or phrases which point to the point in time, the duration, or the frequency of an event. These may be exact, approximate, or even right out vague. Although in our current experiment we restrict ourselves to an eight-day period prior to an event, we chose to create a gross list of all possible temporal expressions we could think of, so that we would not run the risk of overlooking any items and the list can be used on future occasions even when the experimental setting is different. Thus the list also includes temporal expressions that refer to points in time outside the time span under investigation here, such

[6] `http://twiqs.nl`

[7] Ajax, Feyenoord, PSV, FC Twente, AZ Alkmaar, and FC Utrecht.

[8] An analysis of the tweet distribution shows that the eight-day window captures about 98% of the tweets in the larger data set from which it was derived.

as *gisteren* 'yesterday' or *over een maand* 'in a month from now', and items indicating duration or frequency such as *steeds* 'continuously'/'time and again'. No attempt has been made to distinguish between items as regards time reference (future time, past time) as many items can be used in both fashions (compare for example *vanmiddag* in *vanmiddag ga ik naar de wedstrijd* 'this afternoon I'm going to the match' vs *ik ben vanmiddag naar de wedstrijd geweest* 'I went to the match this afternoon'.

The list is quite comprehensive. Among the items included are single words, e.g. adverbs such as *nu* 'now', *zometeen* 'immediately', *straks* 'later on', *vanavond* 'this evening', nouns such as *zondagmiddag* 'Sunday afternoon', and conjunctions such as *voordat* 'before'), but also word combinations and phrases such as *komende woensdag* 'next Wednesday. Temporal expressions of the latter type were obtained by means of a set of 615 seed terms and 70 rules, which generated a total of around 53,000 temporal expressions. In addition, there are a couple of hundred thousand temporal expressions relating the number of minutes, hours, days, or time of day;[9] they include items containing up to 9 words in a single temporal expression. Notwithstanding the impressive number of items included, the list is bound to be incomplete.

We included prepositional phrases rather than single prepositions so as to avoid generating too much noise. Many prepositions have several uses: they can be used to express time, but also for example location. Compare *voor* in *voor drie uur* 'before three o'clock' and *voor het stadion* 'in front of the stadium'. Moreover, prepositions are easily confused with parts of separable verbs which in Dutch are abundant.

Various items on the list are inherently ambiguous and only in one of their senses can be considered temporal expressions. Examples are *week* 'week' but also 'weak' and *dag* 'day' but also 'goodbye'. For items like these, we found that the different senses could fairly easily be distinguished whenever the item was immediately preceded by an adjective such as *komende* and *volgende* (both meaning 'next'). For a few highly frequent items this proved impossible. These are words like *zo* which can be either a temporal adverb ('in a minute'; cf. *zometeen*) or an intensifying adverb ('so'), *dan* 'then' or 'than', and *nog* 'yet' or 'another'. As we have presently no way of distinguishing between the different senses and these items have at best an extremely vague temporal sense so that they cannot be expected to contribute to estimating the time to event, we deciced to discard these.[10]

In order to capture event targeted expressions, we treated domain terms such as *wedstrijd* 'soccer match' as parts of temporal expressions in case they co-occur with a temporal expression.

For the items on the list no provisions were made for handling any kind of spelling variation, with the single exception of a small group of words (including *'s morgens* 'in the morning', *'s middags* 'in the afternoon' and *'s avonds* 'in the evening') which use in their standard spelling the archaic *'s* and abbreviations. As many authors of tweets tend to spell these words as *smorgens*, *smiddags* and *savonds* we decided to include these forms as well.

The items on the list that were obtained through generation include temporal expressions such as *over 3 dagen* 'in 2 days', *nog 5 minuten* 'another 5 minutes', but also fixed temporal expressions such as clock times.[11] The rules handle frequently observed variations in their notation, for example *drie uur* 'three o'clock' may be written in full or as *3:00*, *3:00 uur*, *3 u*, *15.00*, etc.

Table 1 shows example temporal expression estimates and applicable rules. The median estimations are mostly lower than the mean estimations. The distribution of the time to event (TTE) for a single temporal expression often appears to be skewed towards lower values. The final column of the table displays the applicable rules. The first six rules subtract the time the tweet was posted (TT) from an average marker point, heuristically determined, such as 'today 20.00' (i.e. 8 pm) for *vanavond* 'tonight'. The second and third rules from below state a TTE directly, again heuristically set – *over 2 uur* 'in 2 hours' is directly translated to a TTE of 2.

3.3 Evaluation and Baselines

Our approach to TTE estimation makes use of all temporal expressions in our temporal expression list that are found to occur in the tweets. A

[9]For examples see Table 1 and Section 3.3.

[10]Note that *nog* does occur on the list as part of various multiword expressions. Examples are *nog twee dagen* 'another two days' and *nog 10 min* '10 more minutes'.

[11]Dates are presently not covered by our rules but will be added in future.

Temporal Expression	Gloss	Mean TTE	Median TTE	Rule
vandaag	*today*	5.63	3.09	today 15:00 - TT h
vanavond	*tonight*	8.40	4.78	today 20:00 - TT h
morgen	*tomorrow*	20.35	18.54	tomorrow 15:00 - TT h
zondag	*Sunday*	72.99	67.85	Sunday 15:00 - TT h
vandaag 12.30	*today 12.20*	2.90	2.75	today 12:30 - TT h
om 16.30	*at 16.30*	1.28	1.36	today 16:30 - TT h
over 2 uur	*in 2 hours*	6.78	1.97	2 h
nog minder dan 1 u	*within 1 h*	21.43	0.88	1 h
in het weekend	*during the weekend*	90.58	91.70	*No Rule*

Table 1: Examples of temporal expressions and their mean and median TTE estimation from training data. The final column lists the applicable rule, if any. Rules make use of the time of posting (Tweet Time, TT).

match may be for a single item in the list (e.g. *zondag* 'Sunday') or any combination of items (e.g. *zondagmiddag*, *om 14.30 uur*, 'Sunday afternoon', 'at 2.30 pm'). There can be other words in between these expressions. We consider the longest match, from left to right, in case we encounter any overlap.

The experiment adopts a leave-one-out cross-validation setup. Each iteration uses all tweets from 59 events as training data. All tweets from the single held-out event are used as test set.

In the FIN data set there are 42,396 tweets with at least one temporal expression, in the NFI data set this is the case for 27,610 tweets. The number of tweets per event ranges from 66 to 7,152 (median: 402.5; mean 706.6) for the FIN data set and from 41 to 3,936 (median 258; mean 460.1) for the NFI data set.

We calculate the TTE estimations for every tweet that contains at least one of the temporal expression or a combination in the test set. The estimations for the test set are obtained as follows:

1. For each match (a single temporal expression or a combination of temporal expressions) the mean or median value for TTE is used that was learned from the training set;

2. Temporal expressions that denote an exact amount of time are interpreted by means of rules that we henceforth refer to as Exact rules. This applies for example to temporal expressions answering to patterns such as *over N* {*minuut* | *minuten* | *kwartier* | *uur* | *uren* | *dag* | *dagen* | *week*} 'in N {minute | minutes | quarter of an hour | hour | hours | day | days | week}'. Here the TTE is assumed to be the same as the N minutes, days or whatever is mentioned. The rules take precedence over the mean estimates learned from the training set;

3. A second set of rules, referred to as the Dynamic rules, is used to calculate the TTE dynamically, using the temporal expression and the tweet's time stamp. These rules apply to instances such as *zondagmiddag om 3 uur* 'Sunday afternoon at 3 p.m.'. Here we assume that this is a future time reference on the basis of the fact that the tweets were posted prior to the event. With temporal expressions that are underspecified in that they do not provide a specific point in time (hour), we postulate a particular time of day. For example, *vandaag* 'today' is understood as 'today at 3 p.m., *vanavond* 'this evening' as 'this evening at 8 p.m. and *morgenochtend* 'tomorrow morning' as 'tomorrow morning at 10 a.m.'. Again, as was the case with the first set of rules, these rules take precedence over the mean or median estimates learned from the training data.

The results for the estimated TTE are evaluated in terms of the absolute error, i.e. the absolute difference in hours between the estimated TTE and the actual remaining time to the event.

We established two naive baselines: the mean and median TTE measured over all tweets of FIN and NFI datasets. These baselines reflect a best guess when no information is available other than tweet count and TTE of each tweet. The mean TTE is 22.82 hours, and the median TTE is 3.63 hours before an event. The low values of the baselines, especially the low median, reveal the skewedness of the data: most tweets referring to a soccer event are posted in the hours before the event.

4 Results

Table 2 lists the overall mean absolute error (in number of hours) for the different variants. The results are reported separately for each of the two data sets (FIN and NFI) and for both sets aggregated (FIN+NFI). For each of these three variants, the table lists the mean absolute error when only the basic data-driven TTE estimations are used ('Basic'), when the Exact rules are added ('+Ex.'), when the Dynamic rules are added ('+Dyn'), and when both types of rules are added. The coverage of the combination (i.e. the number of tweets that match the expressions and the rules) is listed in the bottom row of the table.

A number of observations can be made. First, all training methods perform substantially better than the two baselines in all conditions. Second, the TTE training method using the median as estimation produces estimations that are about 1 hour more accurate than the mean-based estimations.

Third, adding Dynamic rules has a larger positive effect on prediction error than adding Exact rules. The bottom row in the table indicates that the rules do not increase the coverage of the method substantially. When taken together and added to the basic TTE estimation, the Dynamic and Exact rules do improve over the Basic estimation by two to three hours.

Finally, although the differences are small, Table 2 reveals that training on hashtag-final tweets (FIN) produces slightly better overall results (7.62 hours off at best) than training on hashtag-non-final tweets (8.50 hours off) or the combination (7.99 hours off), despite the fact that the training set is smaller than that of the combination.

In the remainder of this section we report on systems that use all expressions and Exact and Dynamic rules.

Whereas Table 2 displays the overall mean absolute errors of the different variants, Figure 1 displays the results in terms of mean absolute error at different points in time before the event, averaged over periods of one hour, for the two baselines and the FIN+NFI variant with the two training methods (i.e. taking the mean versus the median of the observed TTEs for a particular temporal expression). In contrast to Table 2, in which only a mild difference could be observed between the median and mean variants of training, the figure shows a substantial difference. The estimations of the median training variant are considerably more accurate than the mean variant up to 24 hours before the event, after which the mean variant scores better. By virtue of the fact that the data is skewed (most tweets are posted within a few hours before the event) the two methods attain a similar overall mean absolute error, but it is clear that the median variant produces considerably more accurate predictions when the event is still more than a day away.

While Figure 1 provides insight into the effect of median versus mean-based training with the combined FIN+NFI dataset, we do not know whether training on either of the two subsets is advantageous at different points in time. Table 3 shows the mean absolute error of systems trained with the median variant on the two subsets of tweets, FIN and NFI, as well as the combination FIN+NFI, split into nine time ranges. Interestingly, the combination does not produce the lowest errors close to the event. However, when the event is 24 hours away or more, both the FIN and NFI systems generate increasingly large errors, while the FIN+NFI system continues to make quite accurate predictions, remaining under 10 hours off even for the longest TTEs, confirming what we already observed in Figure 1.

TTE range (h)	FIN	NFI	FIN+NFI
0	**2.58**	3.07	8.51
1–4	**2.38**	2.64	8.71
5–8	**3.02**	3.08	8.94
9–12	**5.20**	5.47	6.57
13–24	5.63	**5.54**	6.09
25–48	13.14	15.59	**5.81**
49–96	17.20	20.72	**6.93**
97–144	30.38	41.18	**6.97**
> 144	55.45	70.08	**9.41**

Table 3: Mean Absolute Error for the FIN, NFI, and FIN+NFI systems in different TTE ranges.

5 Analysis

One of the results observed in Table 2 was the relatively limited role of Exact rules, which were intended to deal with exact temporal expressions such as *nog 5 minuten* '5 more minutes' and *over*

System	FIN				NFI				FIN+NFI			
	Basic	+Ex.	+Dyn.	+Both	Basic	+Ex.	+Dyn.	+Both	Basic	+Ex.	+Dyn.	+Both
Baseline Median	21.09	21.07	21.16	21.14	18.67	18.72	18.79	18.84	20.20	20.20	20.27	20.27
Baseline Mean	27.29	27.29	27.31	27.31	25.49	25.50	25.53	25.55	26.61	26.60	26.63	26.62
Training Median	10.38	10.28	7.68	7.62	11.09	11.04	8.65	8.50	10.61	10.54	8.03	7.99
Training Mean	11.62	11.12	8.73	8.29	12.43	11.99	9.53	9.16	11.95	11.50	9.16	8.76
Coverage	31,221	31,723	32.240	32,740	18,848	19,176	19,734	20,061	52,186	52,919	53,887	54,617

Table 2: Overall Mean Absolute Error for each method: difference in hours between the estimated time to event and the actual time to event, computed separately for the FIN and NFI subsets, and for the combination. For all variants a count of the number of matches is listed in the bottom row.

een uur 'in one hour'. This can be explained by the fact that as long as the temporal expression is related to the event we are targeting, the point in time is denoted exactly by the temporal expression and the estimation obtained from the training data (the 'Basic' performance) will already be accurate, leaving no room for the rules to improve on this. The rules that deal with dynamic temporal expressions, on the other hand, have quite some impact.

As was explained in Section 3.2 our list of temporal expressions was a gross list, including items that were unlikely to occur in our present data. In all we observed 770 of the 53,000 items listed, 955 clock time rule matches, and 764 time expressions which contain number of days, hours, minutes etc. The temporal expressions observed most frequently in our data are:[12] *vandaag* 'today' (10,037), *zondag* 'Sunday' (6,840), *vanavond* 'tonight' (5167), *straks* 'later on' (5,108), *vanmiddag* 'this afternoon' (4,331), *matchday* 'match day' (2,803), *volgende week* 'next week' (1,480) and *zometeen* 'in a minute' (1,405).

Given the skewed distribution of tweets over the eight days prior to the event, it is not surprising to find that nearly all of the most frequent items refer to points in time within close range of the event. Apart from *nu* 'now', all of these are somewhat vague about the exact point in time. There are, however, numerous items such as *om 12:30 uur* 'at half past one' and *over ongeveer 45 minuten* 'in about 45 minutes') which are very specific and therefore tend to appear with middle to low frequencies.[13] And while it is possible to state an exact point in time even when the event is in the more distant future, we find that there is a clear tendency to use underspecified temporal expressions as the event is still some time away. Thus, rather than *volgende week zondag om 14.30 uur* 'next week Sunday at 2.30 p.m.' just *volgende week* is used, which makes it harder to estimate the time to event.

Closer inspection of some of the temporal expressions which yielded large absolute errors suggests that these may be items that refer to subevents rather than the main event (i.e. the match) we are targeting. Examples are *eerst* 'first', *daarna* 'then', *vervolgens* 'next', and *voordat* 'before'.

6 Conclusions and Future Work

We have presented a method for the estimation of the TTE from single tweets referring to a future event. In a case study with Dutch soccer matches, we showed that estimations can be as accurate as about eight hours off, averaged over a time window of eight days. There is some variance in the 60 events on which we tested in a leave-one-out validation setup: errors ranged between 4 and 13 hours, plus one exceptionally badly predicted event with a 34-hour error.

The best system is able to stay within 10 hours of prediction error in the full eight-day window. This best system uses a large set of hand-designed temporal expressions that in a training phase have each been linked to a median TTE with which they occur in a training set. Together with these data-driven TTE estimates, the system uses a set of rules that match on exact and indirect time references. In a comparative experiment we showed that this combination worked better than only having the data-driven estimations.

We then tested whether it was more profitable to train on tweets that had the event hashtag at the end, as this is presumed to be more likely a meta-

[12] The observed frequencies can be found between brackets.

[13] While an expression such as *om 12:30 uur* has a frequency of 116, *nog maar 8 uur en 35 minuten* 'only 8 hours and 35 minutes from now' has a frequency of 1.

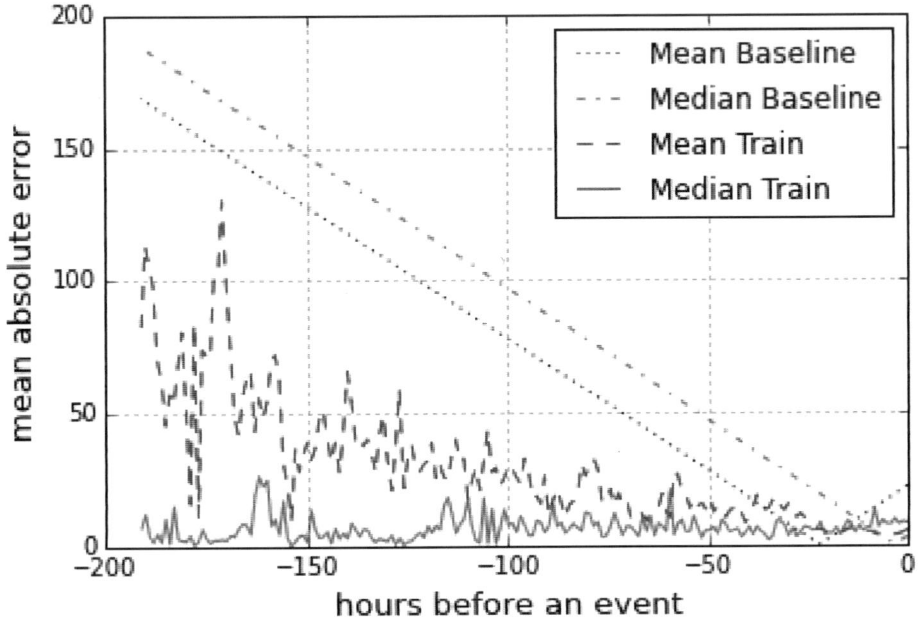

Figure 1: Curves showing the absolute error (in hours) in estimating the time to event over an 8-day period (-192 to 0 hours) prior to the event. The two baselines are compared to the TTE estimation methods using the mean and median variant.

tag, and thus a more reliable clue that the tweet is about the event than when the hashtag is not in final position. Indeed we find that the overall predictions are more accurate, but only in the final hours before the event (when most tweets are posted). 24 hours and earlier before the event it turns out to be better to train both on hashtag-final and hashtag-non-final tweets.

Finally, we observed that the two variants of our method of estimating TTEs for single temporal expressions, taking the mean or the median, leads to dramatically different results, especially when the event is still a few days away—when an accurate time to event is actually desirable. The median-based estimations, which are generally smaller than the mean-based estimations, lead to a system that largely stays under 10 hours of error.

Our study has a number of logical extensions into future research. First, our method is not bound to a single type of event, although we tested it in a controlled setting. With experiments on tweet streams related to different types of events the general applicability of the method could be tested: can we use the trained TTE estimations from our current study, or would we need to retrain per event type?

Second, we hardcoded a limited number of frequent spelling variations, where it would be a more generic solution to rely on a more systematic spelling normalization preprocessing step.

Third, so far we did not focus on determining the relevance of temporal expressions in case there are several time expressions in a single message; we treated all occurred temporal expressions as equally contributing to the estimation. Identifying which temporal expressions are relevant in a single message is studied by Kanhabua et al. (2012).

Finally, our method is limited to temporal expressions. For estimating the time to event on the basis of tweets that do not contain temporal expressions, we could benefit from term-based approaches that consider any word or word n-gram as potentially predictive (Hürriyetoglu et al., 2013).

Acknowledgment

This research was supported by the Dutch national programme COMMIT as part of the Infiniti project.

References

Ricardo Baeza Yates. 2005. Searching the future. In *In ACM SIGIR Workshop on Mathematical/Formal Methods for Information Retrieval (MF/IR 2005).*

Hila Becker, Dan Iter, Mor Naaman, and Luis Gravano. 2012. Identifying content for planned events across social media sites. In *Proceedings of the fifth ACM International Conference on Web Search and Data Mining*, WSDM '12, pages 533–542, New York, NY, USA. ACM.

Gaël Dias, Ricardo Campos, and Alípio Jorge. 2011. Future retrieval: What does the future talk about? In *In Proceedings SIGIR2011 Workshop on Enriching Information Retrieval (ENIR2011).*

Ali Hürriyetoglu, Florian Kunneman, and Antal van den Bosch. 2013. Estimating the time between twitter messages and future events. In *DIR*, pages 20–23.

Adam Jatowt and Ching-man Au Yeung. 2011. Extracting collective expectations about the future from large text collections. In *Proceedings of the 20th ACM International Conference on Information and Knowledge Management*, CIKM '11, pages 1259–1264, New York, NY, USA. ACM.

Nattiya Kanhabua, Sara Romano, and Avaré Stewart. 2012. Identifying relevant temporal expressions for real-world events. In *Proceedings of The SIGIR 2012 Workshop on Time-aware Information Access, Portland, OR.*

Hideki Kawai, Adam Jatowt, Katsumi Tanaka, Kazuo Kunieda, and Keiji Yamada. 2010. Chronoseeker: Search engine for future and past events. In *Proceedings of the 4th International Conference on Uniquitous Information Management and Communication*, ICUIMC '10, pages 25:1–25:10, New York, NY, USA. ACM.

Florian A Kunneman and Antal van den Bosch. 2012. Leveraging unscheduled event prediction through mining scheduled event tweets. *BNAIC 2012 The 24th Benelux Conference on Artificial Intelligence*, page 147.

Taichi Noro, Takashi Inui, Hiroya Takamura, and Manabu Okumura. 2006. Time period identification of events in text. In *Proceedings of the 21st International Conference on Computational Linguistics and the 44th annual meeting of the Association for Computational Linguistics*, ACL-44, pages 1153–1160, Stroudsburg, PA, USA. Association for Computational Linguistics.

Kira Radinsky, Sagie Davidovich, and Shaul Markovitch. 2012. Learning causality for news events prediction. In *Proceedings of the 21st International Conference on World Wide Web*, WWW '12, pages 909–918, New York, NY, USA. ACM.

Alan Ritter, Oren Etzioni Mausam, and Sam Clark. 2012. Open domain event extraction from twitter. In *Proceedings of the 18th ACM SIGKDD International Conference on Knowledge Discovery and Data mining*, KDD '12, pages 1104–1112, New York, NY, USA. ACM.

Takeshi Sakaki, Makoto Okazaki, and Yutaka Matsuo. 2010. Earthquake shakes twitter users: Real-time event detection by social sensors. In *Proceedings of the 19th International Conference on World Wide Web*, pages 851–860. ACM.

Jannik Strötgen and Michael Gertz. 2013. Multilingual and Cross-domain Temporal Tagging. *Language Resources and Evaluation*, 47(2):269–298, Jun.

Hannah Tops, Antal van den Bosch, and Florian Kunneman. 2013. Predicting time-to-event from twitter messages. *BNAIC 2013 The 24th Benelux Conference on Artificial Intelligence*, pages 207–2014.

Wouter Weerkamp and Maarten De Rijke. 2012. Activity prediction: A twitter-based exploration. In *Proceedings of the SIGIR 2012 Workshop on Time-aware Information Access, TAIA-2012*, August.

Andrea Zielinski, Ulrich Bügel, L. Middleton, S. E. Middleton, L. Tokarchuk, K. Watson, and F. Chaves. 2012. Multilingual analysis of twitter news in support of mass emergency events. In A. Abbasi and N. Giesen, editors, *EGU General Assembly Conference Abstracts*, volume 14 of *EGU General Assembly Conference Abstracts*, pages 8085+, April.

Accurate Language Identification of Twitter Messages

Marco Lui and Timothy Baldwin
NICTA VRL
Department of Computing and Information Systems
University of Melbourne, VIC 3010, Australia
mhlui@unimelb.edu.au, tb@ldwin.net

Abstract

We present an evaluation of "off-the-shelf" language identification systems as applied to microblog messages from Twitter. A key challenge is the lack of an adequate corpus of messages annotated for language that reflects the linguistic diversity present on Twitter. We overcome this through a "mostly-automated" approach to gathering language-labeled Twitter messages for evaluating language identification. We present the method to construct this dataset, as well as empirical results over existing datasets and off-the-shelf language identifiers. We also test techniques that have been proposed in the literature to boost language identification performance over Twitter messages. We find that simple voting over three specific systems consistently outperforms any specific system, and achieves state-of-the-art accuracy on the task.

1 Introduction

Twitter[1] has captured the attention of various research communities as a potent data source, because of the immediacy of the information presented, the volume and variability of the data contained, the potential to analyze networking effects within the data, and the ability to (where GPS data is available) geolocate messages (Krishnamurthy et al., 2008). Although individual messages range from inane through mundane right up to insane, the aggregate of these messages can lead to profound insights in real-time. Examples include real-time detection of earthquakes (Sakaki et al., 2010), analysis of the location and prevalence of flu epidemics (Lampos et al., 2010; Culotta, 2010), news event detection (Petrović et al., 2010), and prediction of sporting match outcomes (Sinha et al., 2013).

Text analysis of social media has quickly become one of the "frontier" areas of Natural Language Processing (NLP), with major conferences opening entire tracks for it in recent years. The challenges in NLP for social media are many, stemming primarily from the "noisy" nature of the content. Research indicates that English Twitter in particular is more dissimilar to the kinds of reference corpora used in NLP to date, compared to other forms of social media such as blogs and comments (Baldwin et al., 2013). This has led to the development of techniques to "normalize" Twitter messages (Han et al., 2013), as well as Twitter-specific approaches to conventional NLP tasks such as part-of-speech tagging (Gimpel et al., 2011) and information extraction (Bontcheva et al., 2013). Even so, a precondition of NLP techniques is that the language of the input data is known, and this has led to interest in "language identification" (LangID) of Twitter messages. Research has shown that "off-the-shelf" LangID systems appear to perform fairly well on Twitter (Lui and Baldwin, 2012), but Twitter-specific systems seem to perform better (Carter et al., 2013; Tromp and Pechenizkiy, 2011; Bergsma et al., 2012; Goldszmidt et al., 2013).

Twitter recognizes the utility of language metadata in enabling new applications, and as of March 2013 includes language predictions with results from its API (Roomann-Kurrik, 2013). These predictions are not perfect (see Section 3.2), and at time of writing do not cover some languages (e.g. Romanian). Furthermore, some research groups

[1] http://www.twitter.com

have collected a substantial cache of Twitter data from before the availability of built-in predictions. Motivated by the need to work with monolingual subsets of historical data, we investigate the most practical means of carrying out LangID of Twitter messages, balancing accuracy with ease of implementation. In this work, we present an evaluation of "off-the-shelf" language identifiers, combined with techniques that have been proposed for boosting accuracy on Twitter messages.

A major challenge that we have had to overcome is the lack of annotated data for evaluation. Bergsma et al. (2012) point out that in LangID research on microblog messages to date, only a small number of European languages has been considered. Baldwin and Lui (2010) showed that, when considering full documents, good performance on just European languages does not necessarily imply equally good performance when a larger set of languages is considered. This does not detract from work to date on European languages (Tromp and Pechenizkiy, 2011; Carter et al., 2013), but rather highlights the need for further research in LangID for microblog messages.

Manual annotation of Twitter messages is a challenging and laborious process. Furthermore, Twitter is highly multilingual, making it very difficult to obtain annotators for all of the languages represented. Previous work has attempted to crowdsource part of this process (Bergsma et al., 2012), but such an approach requires substantial monetary investment, as well as care in ensuring the quality of the final annotations. In this paper, we propose an alternative, "mostly-automated" approach to gathering language-labeled Twitter messages for evaluating LangID. A corpus constructed by direct application of automatic LangID to Twitter messages would obviously be unsuitable for evaluating the accuracy of LangID tools. Even with manual post-filtering, the remaining dataset would be biased towards messages that are easy for automated systems to classify correctly. The novelty of our approach is to leverage user identity, allowing us to construct a corpus of language-labeled Twitter messages without using automated tools to determine the languages of the messages. This quality makes the corpus suitable for use in the evaluation of automated LangID of Twitter messages.

Our main contributions are: (1) we provide a manually-labeled dataset of Twitter messages, adding Chinese (zh) and Japanese (ja) to the set of Twitter messages with human annotation for language; (2) we provide a second dataset constructed using a mostly-automated approach, covering 65 languages; (3) we detail the method for constructing the dataset; (4) we provide a comprehensive empirical evaluation of the accuracy of off-the-shelf LangID systems on Twitter messages, using published datasets in addition to the new datasets we have introduced; and (5) we discuss and evaluate a simple voting-based ensemble for LangID, and find that it outperforms any individual system to achieve state-of-the-art results.

2 Background

LangID is the problem of mapping a document onto the language(s) it is written in. The best-known technique classifies documents according to rank order statistics over character n-gram sequences between a document and a global language profile (Cavnar and Trenkle, 1994). Other statistical approaches applied to LangID include Markov models over n-gram frequency profiles (Dunning, 1994), dot products of word frequency vectors (Darnashek, 1995), and string kernels in support vector machines (Kruengkrai et al., 2005). In contrast to purely statistical methods, linguistically-motivated models for LangID have also been proposed, such as the use of stop word lists (Johnson, 1993), where a document is classified according to its degree of overlap with lists for different languages. Other approaches include word and part-of-speech (POS) correlation (Grefenstette, 1995), cross-language tokenization (Giguet, 1995) and grammatical-class models (Dueire Lins and Gonçalves, 2004).

LangID of short strings has attracted recent interest from the research community. Hammarstrom (2007) describes a method that augments a dictionary with an affix table, and tests it over synthetic data derived from a parallel bible corpus. Ceylan and Kim (2009) compare a number of methods for identifying the language of search engine queries of 2 to 3 words. They develop a method which uses a decision tree to integrate outputs from several different LangID approaches. Vatanen et al. (2010) focus on messages of 5–21 characters, using n-gram language models over data drawn from UDHR in a naive Bayes classifier. Carter et al. (2013) focus specifically on LangID in Twitter messages by augmenting standard methods with LangID priors based on a user's previous messages and the content of links embedded in messages, and this is also the method used in `TwitIE` (Bontcheva et al., 2013). Tromp and Pechenizkiy (2011) present a method for LangID of short text messages by means of a graph structure, extending the standard 'bag' model of text to include information about the relative order of tokens. Bergsma et al. (2012) examine LangID for creating language-specific twitter collections, finding that a compressive method trained over out-of-domain data from Wikipedia and standard text corpora performed better than the off-the-shelf language identifiers they tested. Goldszmidt et al. (2013) propose a method based on rank-order statistics, using a bootstrapping process to acquire in-domain training data from unlabeled Twitter messages. Recent work has also put some emphasis on word-level rather than document-level LangID (Yamaguchi and Tanaka-Ishii, 2012; King and Abney, 2013), including research on identifying the language of each word in multilingual online communications (Nguyen and Dogruoz, 2013; Ling et al., 2013). In this paper, we focus on monolingual messages, as despite being simpler, LangID of monolingual Twitter messages is far from solved.

In Section 1, we discussed some work to date on LangID on Twitter data. Some authors have released accompanying datasets: the dataset used by Tromp and Pechenizkiy (2011) was made available in its entirety, consisting of 9066 messages in 6 Western European languages. Other authors have released message identifiers with associated language labels, including Carter et al. (2013), with 5000 identifiers in 5 Western European languages, and Bergsma et al. (2012), providing 13190 identifiers across 9 languages from 3 language families (Arabic, Cyrillic and Devanagari). To date, only the dataset of Tromp and Pechenizkiy (2011) has been used by other researchers (Goldszmidt et al., 2013). With the kind co-operation of the authors, we have obtained the full datasets of Carter et al. (2013) and Bergsma et al. (2012), allowing us to present the most extensive empirical evaluation of LangID of Twitter messages to date. However, the total set of languages covered is still very small. In Section 2.1, we present our own manually-annotated dataset, adding Chinese (zh) and Japanese (ja) to the languages that have manually-annotated data.

	English	Chinese	Japanese
Initial	0.906	0.773	0.989
Post-review	0.930	0.916	0.998

Table 1: Inter-annotator agreement measured using Fleiss' kappa (Fleiss, 1971) over annotations for TWITTER.

2.1 Manual annotation of ZHENJA

A manual approach to constructing a LangID dataset from Twitter data is difficult due to the wide variety of languages present on Twitter — Bergsma et al. (2012) report observing 65 languages in a 10M message sample, and Baldwin et al. (2013) report observing 97 languages in a 1M message sample. While this is encouraging in terms of sourcing data for lower-density languages, the distribution of languages is Zipfian, and the relative proportion of data in most languages is very small. Manually retrieving all available messages in a language would require a native speaker to view and reject a huge number of messages in other languages in order to collect the small number that are written in the target language. We initially attempted this, building ZHENJA, a dataset derived from a set of 5000 messages randomly sampled from a larger body of 622192 messages collected from the Twitter streaming API over a single 24-hour period in August 2010. The messages are a 1% representative sample of the total public messages posted on that day. Each of the 5000 selected messages was annotated by speakers of three languages, English, Japanese and Mandarin Chinese. For each message, three annotators were asked if the message contained any text in languages which they spoke, as well as if it appeared to contain text in (unspecified) languages which they did not speak. The latter label was introduced in order to make a distinction between text in languages not spoken by our annotators (e.g. Portuguese) and text with no linguistic content (e.g. URLs). After the initial annotation, annotators were asked to review messages where there was disagreement, and messages were assigned labels given by a majority of annotators post-review. Inter-annotator agreement (Table 1) is strong for the task: only 20 out of 5000 messages have less than 80% majority in annotations. In many instances, the disagreement was due to messages consisting entirely of a short sequence of hanzi/kanji, which both Chinese and Japanese speakers recognized as valid (these messages are excluded from our set of labeled messages). Out of the 5000 messages, 1953 (39.1%) were labeled as English, 16 were labeled as Chinese (0.3%) and 1047 were labeled as Japanese (20.9%), for a total of 3016 labeled messages.

A total of 8 annotators each invested 2–4 hours in this annotation task, and the final dataset only covers 3 languages (which includes the top-2 highest-density languages in Twitter). Obviously, constructing a dataset of language-labeled Twitter messages is a labor-intensive process, and the lower density the language, the more expensive our methodology becomes (as more and more documents need to be looked over to find documents in the language of interest). Ideally, we would like to be able to use some form of automated LangID to accelerate the process without biasing the data towards easy-to-classify messages.

2.2 A broad-coverage Twitter corpus

Based on our discussion so far, our desiderata for a LangID dataset of Twitter messages are as follows: (1) achieve broader coverage of languages than existing datasets; (2) minimize manual annotation; and (3) avoid bias induced by selecting messages using LangID. (2) and (3) may seem to be conflicting objectives, but we sidestep the problem by first identifying monolingual users, then produce a dataset by sampling messages by these users from a held-out collection.

The overall workflow for constructing a dataset is summarized in Algorithm 1. For each user we consider, we divide all their messages into two disjoint sets. One set (M_u^{main}) is used to determine the language(s) spoken by the user. If only one language is detected, the user is added to a pool of candidate users (U^{accept}). A fixed number of users is sampled for each language (U^{sample}), and for each sampled user a fixed number of messages is sampled from the held-out set ($M_u^{heldout}$) and added to the final dataset. We sample a fixed number of users per language to limit the amount of data in the more-frequent languages, and we only sample a small number of messages per user in order to avoid biasing the dataset towards the linguistic idiosyncrasies of any specific individual. For both sampling steps, if the number of items available is less than the number required, all the available items are returned.

Algorithm 1 uses automated LangID to detect the language of messages in M_u^{main} (line 8). The accuracy of this identifier is not critical, as any misclassifications for a monolingual user would cause them to be rejected, as they would appear multilingual. Hence, the risk of false positives at the user-level LangID is very low. However, incorrectly rejecting users reduces the pool of data available for sampling, so a higher-accuracy solution is preferable. We compared the performance of 8 off-the-shelf (i.e. pre-trained) LangID systems to determine which would be the most suitable for this role.

Algorithm 1 Procedure for building a Twitter LangID dataset

1: $U \leftarrow$ active users
2: $L^{accept}, M^{accept}, U^{accept} \leftarrow \{\}, \{\}, \{\}$
3: **for each** $u \in U$ **do**
4: $\quad M_u \leftarrow$ all messages by user u
5: $\quad M_u^{main}, M_u^{heldout} \leftarrow$ RandomSplit(M_u)
6: $\quad L_u \leftarrow \{\}$
7: $\quad$ **for each** $m \in M_u^{main}$ **do**
8: $\quad\quad l_u \leftarrow$ LangID(m)
9: $\quad\quad$ **if** $l_u \neq$ unknown **then**
10: $\quad\quad\quad L_u \leftarrow L_u \cup \{l_u\}$
11: $\quad\quad$ **end if**
12: $\quad$ **end for**
13: $\quad$ **if** $len(L_u) = 1$ **then**
14: $\quad\quad U^{accept} \leftarrow U^{accept} \cup \{(u, L_u)\}$
15: $\quad\quad L^{accept} \leftarrow L^{accept} \cup L_u$
16: $\quad$ **end if**
17: **end for**
18: **for each** $l \in L_{accept}$ **do**
19: $\quad U^{sample} \leftarrow$ Sample(U_l^{accept}, K)
20: $\quad$ **for each** $u \in U^{sample}$ **do**
21: $\quad\quad M^{sample} \leftarrow$ Sample($M_u^{heldout}, N$)
22: $\quad\quad M^{accept} \leftarrow M^{accept} \cup \{(M^{sample}, l)\}$
23: $\quad$ **end for**
24: **end for**
25: **return** M^{accept}

`langid.py` (Lui and Baldwin, 2012): an n-gram feature set selected using data from multiple sources, combined with a multinomial naive Bayes classifier.

`CLD2` (McCandless, 2010): the language identifier embedded in the Chrome web browser;[2] it uses a naive Bayes classifier and script-specific tokenization strategies.

`LangDetect` (Nakatani, 2010): a naive Bayes classifier, using a character n-gram based representation without feature selection, with a set of normalization heuristics to improve accuracy.

`LDIG` (Nakatani, 2012): a Twitter-specific LangID tool, which uses a document representation based on tries, combined with normalization

[2] `http://www.google.com/chrome`

heuristics and Bayesian classification, trained on Twitter data.

`whatlang` (Brown, 2013): a vector-space model with per-feature weighting over character n-grams.

`YALI` (Majliš, 2012): computes a per-language score using the relative frequency of a set of byte n-grams selected by term frequency.

`TextCat` (Scheelen, 2003); an implementation of Cavnar and Trenkle (1994), which uses an adhoc rank-order statistic over character n-grams.

`MSR-LID` (Goldszmidt et al., 2013): based on rank-order statistics over character n-grams, and Spearman's ρ to measure correlation. Twitter-specific training data is acquired through a bootstrapping approach. We use the 49-language model provided by the authors, and the best parameters reported in the paper.

We investigated the performance of the systems using manually-labeled datasets of Twitter messages (Table 2), including the ZHENJA set described in Section 2.1.[3] We find that all the systems tested perform well on TROMP, with the exception of `TextCat`. CARTER covers a very similar set of languages to TROMP, yet all systems consistently perform worse on it. This suggests that TROMP is biased towards messages that LangID systems are likely to identify correctly (also observed by Goldszmidt et al. (2013)). This is due in part to the post-processing applied to the messages, but also suggests a bias in how messages were selected. `LDIG` is the best performer on TROMP and CARTER, albeit falling slightly short of the 99.1% accuracy reported by the author (Nakatani, 2012). However, it is only trained on 17 languages and thus is not able to fully support BERGSMA and ZHENJA, and so we cannot draw any conclusions on whether the method will generalize well to more languages. The system that supports the most languages by far is `whatlang`, but as a result its accuracy on Twitter messages suffers. Manual analysis suggests this is due to Twitter-specific "noise" tipping the model in favor of lower-density languages. On BERGSMA, `LangDetect` is the best performer, likely due to its specific heuristics for distinguishing certain language pairs (Nakatani, 2010), which happen to be present in the BERGSMA dataset. Overall, in their off-the-shelf configuration, only three systems (`langid.py`, `CLD2`, `LangDetect`) perform consistently well on LangID of Twitter messages. Even so, the macro-averaged F-Scores observed were as low as 83%, indicating that whilst performance is good, the problem of LangID of Twitter messages is far from solved.

Given that the set of languages covered and accuracy varies between systems, we investigated a simple voting-based approach to combining the predictions. For each dataset, we considered all combinations of 3, 5, and 7 systems, combining the predictions using a simple majority vote. The single-best combination for each dataset is reported in Table 3. In all cases, the macro-averaged F-score is improved upon, showing the effectiveness of the voting approach. Hence, for purposes of LangID in Algorithm 1, we chose to use a majority-vote ensemble of `langid.py`, `CLD2` and `LangDetect`, a combination that generally performs well on all datasets.[4] Where all 3 systems disagree, the message is labeled as unknown, which does not count as a separate language for determining if a user is multilingual, mitigating the risk of wrongly rejecting a monolingual user due to misclassifying a particular message. This ensemble is hereafter referred to as VOTING.

To build our final dataset, we collected all messages by active users from the 1% feed made available by Twitter over the course of 31 days, between 8 January 2012 and 7 February 2012. We deemed users active if they had posted at least 5 messages in a single day on at least 7 different days in the 31-day period we collected data for. This gave us a set of approximately 2M users. For each user, we partitioned their messages (RandomSplit in Algorithm 1) by selecting one day at random. All of the messages posted by the user on this day were treated as heldout data ($M_u^{heldout}$), and the remainder of the user's messages (M_u^{main}) were used to determine the language(s) spoken by the user. The day chosen was randomly selected per-user to avoid any bias that may be introduced by messages from a particular day or date. Of the active users, we identified 85.0% to be monolingual, covering a set of 65 languages. 50.6% of these users spoke English (en), 14.1% spoke Japanese (ja), and 13.0% spoke Portuguese (pt); this user-level

[3]We do not limit the comparison to languages supported by each system as this would bias evaluation towards systems that support few languages that are easy to discriminate.

[4]`MSR-LID` was excluded due to technical difficulties in applying it to a large collection of messages because of its oversized model.

Dataset	langid.py	CLD2	LangDetect	LDIG	whatlang	YALI	TextCat	MSR-LID
TROMP	0.983	0.972	0.959	0.986	0.950	0.911	0.814	0.983
CARTER	0.917	0.902	0.891	0.943	0.834	0.824	0.510	0.927
BERGSMA	0.847	0.911	0.923	*0.000*	0.719	*0.428*	*0.046*	*0.546*
ZHENJA	0.871	0.884	0.831	*0.315*	0.622	0.877	0.313	0.848

Table 2: Macro-averaged F-Score on manually-annotated Twitter datasets. *Italics* denotes results where the dataset contains languages not supported by the identifier.

Dataset	Single Best		Voting		3-System
	System	F-Score	Systems	F-Score	F-Score
TROMP	LDIG	0.986	CLD2, MSR-LID, LDIG	0.992	0.986
CARTER	LDIG	0.943	MSR-LID, langid.py, LDIG	0.948	0.927
BERGSMA	LangDetect	0.923	CLD2, LangDetect, langid.py	0.935	0.935
ZHENJA	CLD2	0.884	CLD2, MSR-LID, LDIG, YALI, langid.py	0.969	0.941

Table 3: System combination by majority voting. All combinations of 3, 5 and 7 systems were considered. For each dataset, we report the single-best system, the best combination, and F-score of the majority-vote combination of langid.py, CLD2 and LangDetect.

language distribution largely mirrors the message-level language distribution reported by Baldwin et al. (2013) and others. From this set of users, we randomly selected up to 100 users per language, leaving us with a pool of 26011 held-out messages from 2914 users. Manual inspection of these messages revealed a number of English messages mislabeled with another language, indicating that even predominantly monolingual users occasionally introduce English into their online communications. Such messages are generally entirely English, with code-switching (i.e. multiple languages in the same message) very rarely observed. In order to eliminate mislabeled messages, we applied all 8 systems to this pool of 26011 messages. Where at least 5 systems agree and the predicted language does not match the user's language, we discarded the message. Where 3 or 4 systems agree, we manually inspected the messages and eliminated those that were clearly mislabeled (this is the only manual step in the construction of this dataset). Overall, we retained 24220 messages (93.1%). From these, we sampled up to 5 messages per unique user, producing a final dataset of 14178 messages across 65 languages (hereafter referred to as the TWITUSER dataset).

3 Evaluating off-the-shelf language identifiers on Twitter

Given TWITUSER, our broad-coverage Twitter corpus, we return to the task of examining the performance of the off-the-shelf LangID systems we discussed in Section 2.2 (Table 4, left side). In terms of macro-averaged F-Score across the full set of 65 languages, CLD2 is the single best-performing system. Unlike langid.py and LangDetect, CLD2 does not always produce a prediction, and instead has an in-built threshold for it to output a prediction of "unknown". This is reflected in the elevated precision, at the expense of decreased recall and message-level accuracy. Systems like langid.py which always make a prediction have reduced precision, balanced by increased recall and message-level accuracy. As with the manually-annotated datasets, we experimented with a simple voting-based approach to combining multiple classifiers. We again experimented with all possible combinations of 3, 5 and 7 classifiers, and found that on TWITUSER, a majority-vote ensemble of CLD2, langid.py and LangDetect attains the best macro-averaged F-Score, and also outperforms any individual system on all of the metrics considered. We note that this is exactly the VOTING ensemble of Section 2.2, validating its choice as LangID(m) in Algorithm 1.

3.1 Adapting off-the-shelf LangID to Twitter

Tromp and Pechenizkiy (2011) propose to remove links, usernames, hashtags and smilies before attempting LangID, as they are Twitter specific. We experimented with applying this cleaning procedure to each message body before passing it to our off-the-shelf systems (Table 4, right side). For LDIG and MSR-LID, the results are exactly the same with and without cleaning. These two systems are specifically targeted at Twitter messages, and thus may include a similar normalization as part of their processing pipeline. This also suggests that the systems do not leverage this Twitter-

Tool	Without Cleaning				With Cleaning			
	P	R	F	Acc	P	R	F	Acc
`langid.py`	0.767	0.861	0.770	0.842	0.759	0.861	0.766	0.840
`CLD2`	0.852	0.814	0.806	0.775	0.866	0.823	0.820	0.780
`LangDetect`	0.618	0.680	0.626	0.839	0.623	0.687	0.634	0.854
`LDIG`	0.167	0.239	0.189	0.447	0.167	0.239	0.189	0.447
`whatlang`	0.749	0.655	0.663	0.624	0.739	0.667	0.663	0.623
`YALI`	0.441	0.564	0.438	0.710	0.449	0.560	0.443	0.705
`TextCat`	0.327	0.245	0.197	0.257	0.316	0.295	0.230	0.316
`MSR-LID`	0.533	0.609	0.536	0.848	0.533	0.609	0.536	0.848
VOTING	0.920	0.876	0.887	0.861	0.919	0.883	0.889	0.868

Table 4: Macro-averaged Precision/Recall/F-Score, as well as message-level accuracy for each system on TWITUSER. The right side of the table reports results after applying message-level cleaning (Tromp and Pechenizkiy, 2011).

specific content in making predictions. Other systems generally show a small improvement with cleaning, except for `langid.py`. The VOTING ensemble also benefits from cleaning, due to the improvement in two of its component classifiers (`CLD2` and `LangDetect`). This cleaning procedure is trivial to implement, so despite the improvement being small, it may be worth implementing if adapting off-the-shelf language identifiers to Twitter messages.

Goldszmidt et al. (2013) suggest bootstrapping a Twitter-specific language identifier using an off-the-shelf language identifier and an unlabeled collection of Twitter messages. We tested this approach, using the 3 systems that provide tools to generate new models from labeled data (`LangDetect`, `langid.py` and `TextCat`). We constructed bootstrap collections by: (1) using the off-the-shelf tools to directly identify the language of messages; and (2) using Algorithm 1. Overall, the bootstrapped identifiers are not better than their off-the-shelf counterparts. For `TextCat` there is an increase in accuracy using bootstrapped models, but the accuracy of `TextCat` with bootstrapped models is still inferior to `LangDetect` and `langid.py` in their off-the-shelf configuration. For `LangDetect`, utilizing bootstrapped models does not always increase the accuracy of LangID of Twitter messages. Where it does help, the bootstrap collections that are effective vary with the target dataset. For `langid.py`, none of the bootstrapped models outperformed the off-the-shelf model. This suggests that for LangID, the same features that are predictive of language in other domains are equally applicable to Twitter messages, and that the cross-domain feature selection procedure proposed utilized by `langid.py` (Lui and Baldwin, 2011) is able to identify these features effectively.

Dataset	Period	Proportion
CARTER	Jan – Apr 2010	76.4%
BERGSMA	May 2007 – Feb 2012	92.2%
TWITUSER	Jan – Feb 2012	79.7%

Table 5: Proportion of messages from each dataset that were still accessible as of August 2013.

Bontcheva et al. (2013) report positive results from the integration of LangID priors (Carter et al., 2013), but we did not experiment with them, as the calculation of priors is relatively expensive compared to the other adaptations we have considered, in terms of both run time and developer effort. Furthermore, there is a number of open issues that are likely to affect the effectiveness of the priors, such as the size and the scope of the message collection used to determine the prior. This is an interesting avenue of future work but is beyond the scope of this particular paper. However, we observe that priors based on user identity (e.g the "Blogger" prior) are likely to be artificially effective on TWITUSER, because the messages have been sampled from users that we have identified as monolingual.

3.2 Twitter API predictions

For CARTER, BERGSMA and TWITUSER, we have access to the original identifiers for each message, which use used to download the messages via the Twitter API.[5] Table 5 reports the proportion of each dataset that is still accessible as of August 2013. For the messages that we were able to recover, the full response from the API now includes language predictions. We do not report quantitative results on the accuracy of the Twitter API predictions as the Twitter API terms of ser-

[5] `http://dev.twitter.com`

vice forbid benchmarking ("You will not attempt ... to ... use or access the Twitter API ... for ... benchmarking or competitive purposes"). Furthermore, any results would be impossible to replicate: the set of messages that are accessible is likely to continue to decrease, and the accuracy of Twitter's predictions may vary as updates are made to the API.

Error analysis of the language predictions provided by the Twitter API shows that at the time of writing, for the languages supported the accuracy of the Twitter API is not substantially better than the best off-the-shelf language identifiers we examined in this paper. However, about a quarter of the languages present in TWITUSER are never offered as predictions. This has implications for the precision of LangID in other languages: one notable example is poor precision in Italian, due to some Romanian messages being identified as Italian (no messages are identified as Romanian). This suggests that caution must be taken in taking the language predictions offered by the Twitter API as goldstandard. The accuracy of the predictions is not perfect, and highlights the need for further research into improving the scope and accuracy of LangID for Twitter messages.

4 Conclusion

In this paper, we presented ZHENJA and TWITUSER, two novel datasets of language-labeled Twitter messages. ZHENJA is constructed using a conventional manual annotation approach, whereas TWITUSER is constructed using a novel mostly-automated method that leverages user identity. Using these new datasets alongside three previously-published datasets, we compared 8 off-the-shelf LangID systems over Twitter messages, and found that a simple majority vote across three specific systems (`CLD2`, `langid.py`, `LangDetect`) consistently outperforms any individual system. We also found that removing Twitter-specific content from messages improves the performance of off-the-shelf systems. We reported that the predictions provided by the Twitter API are not better than state-of-the-art off-the-shelf systems, and that a number of languages in use on Twitter appear to be unsupported by the Twitter API, underscoring the need for further research to broaden the scope and accuracy of language identification from Twitter messages.

Acknowledgments

NICTA is funded by the Australian Government as represented by the Department of Broadband, Communications and the Digital Economy and the Australian Research Council through the ICT Centre of Excellence program.

References

Timothy Baldwin and Marco Lui. 2010. Language identification: The long and the short of the matter. In *Proceedings of Human Language Technologies: The 11th Annual Conference of the North American Chapter of the Association for Computational Linguistics (NAACL HLT 2010)*, pages 229–237, Los Angeles, USA.

Timothy Baldwin, Paul Cook, Marco Lui, Andrew MacKinlay, and Li Wang. 2013. How noisy social media text, how diffrnt social media sources? In *Proceedings of the 6th International Joint Conference on Natural Language Processing (IJCNLP 2013)*, Nagoya, Japan.

Shane Bergsma, Paul McNamee, Mossaab Bagdouri, Clayton Fink, and Theresa Wilson. 2012. Language identification for creating language-specific Twitter collections. In *Proceedings the Second Workshop on Language in Social Media (LSM2012)*, pages 65–74, Montréal, Canada.

Kalina Bontcheva, Leon Derczynski, Adam Funk, Mark A. Greenwood, Diana Maynard, and Niraj Aswani. 2013. TwitIE: An open-source information extraction pipeline for microblog text. In *Proceedings of Recent Advances in Natural Language Processing (RANLP 2013)*, Hissar, Buglaria.

Ralf Brown. 2013. Selecting and weighting n-grams to identify 1100 languages. In *Proceedings of the 16th international conference on text, speech and dialogue (TSD 2013)*, Plzeň, Czech Republic.

Simon Carter, Wouter Weerkamp, and Manos Tsagkias. 2013. Microblog language identification: Overcoming the limitations of short, unedited and idiomatic text. *Language Resources and Evaluation*, pages 1–21.

William B. Cavnar and John M. Trenkle. 1994. N-gram-based text categorization. In *Proceedings of the Third Symposium on Document Analysis and Information Retrieval*, pages 161–175, Las Vegas, USA.

Hakan Ceylan and Yookyung Kim. 2009. Language identification of search engine queries. In *Proceedings of the Joint Conference of the 47th Annual Meeting of the ACL and the 4th International Joint Conference on Natural Language Processing of the AFNLP*, pages 1066–1074, Singapore.

Aron Culotta. 2010. Towards detecting influenza epidemics by analyzing Twitter messages. In *Proceedings of the KDD Workshop on Social Media Analytics*.

Marc Darnashek. 1995. Gauging similarity with n-grams: Language-independent categorization of text. *Science*, 267:843–848.

Rafael Dueire Lins and Paulo Gonçalves. 2004. Automatic language identification of written texts. In *Proceedings of the 2004 ACM Symposium on Applied Computing (SAC 2004)*, pages 1128–1133, Nicosia, Cyprus.

Ted Dunning. 1994. Statistical identification of language. Technical Report MCCS 940-273, Computing Research Laboratory, New Mexico State University.

Joseph L. Fleiss. 1971. Measuring nominal scale agreement among many raters. *Psychological Bulletin*, 76(5):378–382.

Emmanuel Giguet. 1995. Categorisation according to language: A step toward combining linguistic knowledge and statistical learning. In *Proceedings of the 4th International Workshop on Parsing Technologies (IWPT-1995)*, Prague, Czech Republic.

Kevin Gimpel, Nathan Schneider, Brendan O'Connor, Dipanjan Das, Daniel Mills, Jacob Eisenstein, Michael Heilman, Dani Yogatama, Jeffrey Flanigan, and Noah A. Smith. 2011. Part-of-speech tagging for Twitter: Annotation, features, and experiments. In *Proceedings of the 49th Annual Meeting of the Association for Computational Linguistics: Human Language Technologies (ACL HLT 2011)*, pages 42–47, Portland, USA.

Moises Goldszmidt, Marc Najork, and Stelios Paparizos. 2013. Boot-strapping language identifiers for short colloquial postings. In *Proceedings of the European Conference on Machine Learning and Principles and Practice of Knowledge Discovery in Databases (ECMLPKDD 2013)*, Prague, Czech Republic.

Gregory Grefenstette. 1995. Comparing two language identification schemes. In *Proceedings of Analisi Statistica dei Dati Testuali (JADT)*, pages 263–268, Rome, Italy.

Harald Hammarstrom. 2007. A Fine-Grained Model for Language Identication. In *Proceedings of Improving Non English Web Searching (iNEWS07)*, pages 14–20.

Bo Han, Paul Cook, and Timothy Baldwin. 2013. Lexical normalization for social media text. *ACM Trans. Intell. Syst. Technol.*, 4(1):5:1–5:27, February.

Stephen Johnson. 1993. Solving the problem of language recognition. Technical report, School of Computer Studies, University of Leeds.

Ben King and Steven Abney. 2013. Labeling the languages of words in mixed-language documents using weakly supervised methods. In *Proceedings of the 2013 Conference of the North American Chapter of the Association for Computational Linguistics: Human Language Technologies*, pages 1110–1119, Atlanta, Georgia.

Balachander Krishnamurthy, Phillipa Gill, and Martin Arlitt. 2008. A few chirps about Twitter. In *Proceedings of the First Workshop on Online Social Networks (WOSN 2008)*, pages 19–24, Seattle, USA.

Canasai Kruengkrai, Prapass Srichaivattana, Virach Sornlertlamvanich, and Hitoshi Isahara. 2005. Language identification based on string kernels. In *Proceedings of the 5th International Symposium on Communications and Information Technologies (ISCIT-2005)*, pages 896–899, Beijing, China.

Vasileios Lampos, Tijl De Bie, and Nello Cristianini. 2010. Flu Detector – tracking epidemics on Twitter. In *Proceedings of the European Conference on Machine Learning and Principles and Practice of Knowledge Discovery in Databases (ECML PKDD 2010)*, pages 599–602, Barcelona, Spain.

Wang Ling, Guang Xiang, Chris Dyer, Alan Black, and Isabel Trancoso. 2013. Microblogs as parallel corpora. In *Proceedings of the 51st Annual Meeting of the Association for Computational Linguistics (Volume 1: Long Papers)*, pages 176–186, Sofia, Bulgaria.

Marco Lui and Timothy Baldwin. 2011. Cross-domain feature selection for language identification. In *Proceedings of the 5th International Joint Conference on Natural Language Processing (IJCNLP 2011)*, pages 553–561, Chiang Mai, Thailand.

Marco Lui and Timothy Baldwin. 2012. langid.py: An off-the-shelf language identification tool. In *Proceedings of the 50th Annual Meeting of the Association for Computational Linguistics (ACL 2012) Demo Session*, pages 25–30, Jeju, Republic of Korea.

Martin Majliš. 2012. Yet another language identifier. In *Proceedings of the Student Research Workshop at the 13th Conference of the European Chapter of the Association for Computational Linguistics*, pages 46–54, Avignon, France.

Michael McCandless. 2010. Accuracy and performance of google's compact language detector. blog post. available at `http://blog.mikemccandless.com/2011/10/accuracy-and-performance-of-googles.html`.

Shuyo Nakatani. 2010. Language detection library (slides). `http://www.slideshare.net/shuyo/language-detection-library-for-java`. Retrieved on 21/06/2013.

Shuyo Nakatani. 2012. Short text language detection with infinity-gram. blog post. available at `http://shuyo.wordpress.com/2012/05/17/short-text-language-detection-with-infinity-gram/`.

Dong Nguyen and A. Seza Dogruoz. 2013. Word level language identification in online multilingual communication. In *Proceedings of the 2013 Conference on Empirical Methods in Natural Language Processing*, pages 857–862, Seattle, USA.

S. Petrović, Miles Osborne, and Victor Lavrenko. 2010. Streaming first story detection with application to twitter. In *Proceedings of Human Language Technologies: The 11th Annual Conference of the North American Chapter of the Association for Computational Linguistics (NAACL HLT 2010)*, pages 181–189, Los Angeles, USA.

Arne Roomann-Kurrik. 2013. Introducing new metadata fro tweets. blog post. available at `https://dev.twitter.com/blog/introducing-new-metadata-for-tweets`.

Takeshi Sakaki, Makoto Okazaki, and Yutaka Matsuo. 2010. Earthquake shakes Twitter users: real-time event detection by social sensors. In *Proceedings of the 19th International Conference on the World Wide Web (WWW 2010)*, pages 851–860, Raleigh, USA.

Frank Scheelen, 2003. *libtextcat*. Software available at `http://software.wise-guys.nl/libtextcat/`.

Shiladitya Sinha, Chris Dyer, Kevin Gimpel, and Noah A. Smith. 2013. Predicting the NFL using Twitter. In *Proceedings of the ECML/PKDD Workshop on Machine Learning and Data Mining for Sports Analytics*, Prague, Czech Republic.

Erik Tromp and Mykola Pechenizkiy. 2011. Graph-based n-gram language identification on short texts. In *Proceedings of Benelearn 2011*, pages 27–35, The Hague, Netherlands.

Tommi Vatanen, Jaakko J. Vayrynen, and Sami Virpioja. 2010. Language identification of short text segments with n-gram models. In *Proceedings of the 7th International Conference on Language Resources and Evaluation (LREC 2010)*, pages 3423–3430.

Hiroshi Yamaguchi and Kumiko Tanaka-Ishii. 2012. Text segmentation by language using minimum description length. In *Proceedings the 50th Annual Meeting of the Association for Computational Linguistics (Volume 1: Long Papers)*, pages 969–978, Jeju Island, Korea.

The (Un)Predictability of Emotional Hashtags in Twitter

Florian Kunneman*, **Christine Liebrecht****, **and Antal van den Bosch***

*Centre for Language Studies
Radboud University Nijmegen
{f.kunneman,a.vandenbosch}@let.ru.nl

**Faculty of Social and Behavioral Sciences
University of Amsterdam
c.c.liebrecht@uva.nl

Abstract

Hashtags in Twitter posts may carry different semantic payloads. Their dual form (word and label) may serve to categorize the tweet, but may also add content to the message, or strengthen it. Some hashtags are related to emotions. In a study on emotional hashtags in Dutch Twitter posts we employ machine learning classifiers to test to what extent tweets that are stripped from their hashtag could be reassigned to this hashtag. About half of the 24 tested hashtags can be predicted with AUC scores of .80 or higher. However, when we apply the three best-performing classifiers to unseen tweets that do not carry the hashtag but might have carried it according to human annotators, the classifiers manage to attain a precision-at-250 of .7 for only two of the hashtags. We observe that some hashtags are predictable from their tweets, and strengthen the emotion already expressed in the tweets. Other hashtags are added to messages that do not predict them, presumably to provide emotional information that was not yet in the tweet.

1 Introduction

Since the launch of Twitter in 2006 the microblogging service has proven to be a valuable source of research on the linguistic expression of sentiment and affect. Sentiments and emotions are important aspects of status updates and conversations in Twitter messages (Ritter et al., 2010; Dann, 2010). Many Twitter messages (tweets) express an emotion of the sender: according to Roberts *et al.* (2012), 43 percent of the 7,000 tweets they collected are an emotional expression. Automatically detecting the emotion in tweets is key to understand the sentiment underlying real world events and topics.

Potentially, Twitter offers a vast amount of data to exploit for the construction of computational models able to detect certain sentiments or emotions in unseen tweets. Yet, in the typical scenario of applying supervised machine learning classifiers, some annotation effort will be required to label sentiments and emotions reliably. Currently there are two main approaches to labeling tweets. The first is the annotation of data by human experts (Alm et al., 2005; Aman and Szpakowicz, 2007). This approach is known to result in high-precision annotated data, but is labor-intensive and time-consuming.

The second approach is to use the annotations that Twitter users themselves add to a tweet: hashtags. A hashtag (a word prefixed by the typographical hashmark #) is an explicitly marked keyword that may also serve as a word in the context of the other non-tagged words of the post. The usage of a hashtag in Twitter serves many purposes beyond mere categorization, most of which are conversational (Huang et al., 2010). Hashtags expressing emotions are often used in tweets and are therefore potentially useful annotations for training data. Wang et al. (2012) state that annotating interpretative labels by humans other than the author is not as reliable as having the data annotated by the author himself. As far as emotions can be self-observed and self-reported, authors arguably have the best information about their own emotions. Following González-Ibáñez et al. (2011), Mohammad (2012) presents several experiments to validate that the emotional labels in tweets are consistent and match intuitions of trained judges.

Therefore, using hashtags as annotated training data may be useful for generating emotion detectors. Yet, not all hashtags are equally suitable for this task. Even a high level of consistency and predictability in hashtag usage might not be sufficient.

Mohammad (2012) argues that emotion hashtags are included in tweets by users in two different ways. First, the hashtag can *strengthen* the emotion already present in the tweet. By adding the hashtag in for example 'I hate making homework #fml' (#fml is an acronym for 'fuck my life'), the sender reflects on his own negative message and strengthens it with an abbreviated expletive.

Second, the hashtag can *add* emotion to the message in order to avoid miscommunication. Lacking the richness of non-verbal cues in face-to-face communication, as well as the space to elaborate, attenuate, or add nuance, users of Twitter might deploy hashtags to signify the intention or emotion of their message. In the expression 'Making homework #fml' for example, a Twitter user adds sentiment to the message to clarify his negative attitude towards the described activity. Mohammad (2012, p. 248) formulates the second function of a hashtag as follows: 'reading just the message before the hashtag does not convey the emotions of the tweeter. Here, the hashtag provides information not present (implicitly or explicitly) in the rest of the message.'

Arguably, hashtags that are most often used to add emotion to an otherwise emotionally neutral message (the second function) will not provide proper training data for the detection of the emotion linked to the hashtag; only examples of the first function may serve that purpose. As this information is not explicit, the suitability of a hashtag as an emotion label needs to be revealed in another way. We propose an automatic method that uses machine-learning-based text classification. We put this method into practice for a number of hashtags expressing emotion in Dutch tweets. The novel contribution of this research lies in the fact that we offer an objective, empirical handle of the two usages of emotion hashtags as formulated by Mohammad (2012). Furthermore, we exemplify a new type of study that tests our hypothesis in the realistic scenario of testing on a full day of streaming tweets with no filtering.

2 Related research

Leveraging uncontrolled labeling to obtain large amounts of training data is referred to as *distant supervision* (Mintz et al., 2009). With its conventions for hashtags as extra-linguistic markers, Twitter is a potentially suitable platform for implementing classification based on distant supervision. In the field of sentiment analysis, Pak and Paroubek (2010) and Go, Bhayani and Huang (2009) select emoticons representing positive and negative sentiment to collect tweets with either of the polarities. Several studies focusing on the specific task of emotion detection in Twitter also apply distant supervision. The studies in which it is applied vary in a number of ways. First, the type of markers by which data is collected differs. Most often only hashtags are used, occasionally combined with emoticons. Davidov, Tsur and Rappoport (2010) use hashtags and emoticons as distinct prediction labels and find that they are equally useful. Suttles and Ide (2013) compare the usage of hashtags, emoticons, and emoji[1], and find that emoji form a valuable addition.

Second, the selection of emotions and markers differs. In many of the studies a predefined set of emotions form the starting point for the selection of markers and collection of data. Emotions can be classified according to a set of basic emotions, such as Ekman's (Ekman, 1971) six basic emotions (happiness, sadness, anger, fear, surprise, and disgust), or the bipolar emotions defined by Plutchik's wheel of emotions (Plutchik, 1980) which are based on the basic emotions anger, fear, sadness, disgust, surprise, anticipation, trust, and joy. The majority of the studies rely on such categorizations (Mohammad, 2012; Suttles and Ide, 2013; Wang et al., 2012).

In spite of the interesting findings in such studies, basic emotions do not tell the whole story; tweets may contain multiple basic emotions combining into more complex emotions (Roberts et al., 2012; Kamvar and Harris, 2011). Furthermore, by selecting a set of hashtags that are assumed to match the same emotion, the potential variation in the usage of specific hashtags by users is ignored. A different approach is to select single hashtags expressing emotion as starting points, regardless of their theoretical status. Davidov et.al. (2010) select frequent hashtags from a large twitter corpus and let annotators judge the strength of their sentiment. The fifty hashtags with the strongest sentiment are used as label. In our research, we also single out hashtags, focusing on a set of hashtags that are linked to emotions, some of which are complex.

Third, the way in which a classifier is trained and tested differs. In some studies multi-class

[1] http://en.wikipedia.org/wiki/Emoji

classification is performed, distinguishing the different target emotions and optionally an emotionally neutral class (Purver and Battersby, 2012; Wang et al., 2012). The multitude of classes, class imbalance, and the possibility of single tweets conveying multiple emotions make this a challenging task. The alternative is to train a binary classifier for each emotion (Mohammad, 2012; Qadir and Riloff, 2013; Suttles and Ide, 2013), deciding for each unseen tweet whether it conveys the trained emotion. We apply the latter type of classification.

The fourth and final variation is the way in which classification is evaluated. In the discussed papers, evaluation is either performed in a ten-fold cross-validation setting or by testing the trained classifier on a small, manually annotated set of tweets. We deviate from these approaches by testing our classifiers on a large set of uncontrolled tweets gathered in a single day, thereby approximating the real world scenario in which emotion detection is applied to the stream of incoming tweets.

3 Approach

Our approach is to train a machine learning classifier on tweets containing an emotion-bearing hashtag and an equal amount of random tweets as counter-examples, resulting in a balanced binary classifier for the hashtag (which itself is stripped from the tweet and purely considered as a label). The classifier is then run on a large sample of tweets, deciding which of the tweets might fit the target hashtag. As some of these test tweets actually contain the hashtag, a first evaluation is to score the amount of tweets of which the hashtag is correctly predicted by the classifier, when this hashtag is hidden from the classifier. Second, the tweets not containing the hashtag can be ranked by classifier confidence for the hashtag class, after which the 250 highest ranked tweets are scored by human annotators, who judge whether these tweets convey the emotion that is linked to the hashtag.

This approach is based on the assumption that a hashtag as a label for emotion detection requires two relations between the hashtag and the text with which it co-occurs in tweets:

1. The context in which users include the hashtag is to a certain extent consistent with the hashtag. In other words, the context (the tweet) would predict the hashtag. If this is the case, our classifier should score well on the retrieval of unseen tweets containing the hashtag (the first evaluation). Consistency can arise from many different types of features, ranging from topical words to emotion-bearing words.

2. The emotion that is denoted by the hashtag should be reflected in the words surrounding it. Hashtags that add emotion to an otherwise neutral message are inappropriate as annotation label for emotion detection. By evaluating retrieved tweets that do not contain the hashtag on the conveyed *emotion* (instead of their possible fit with the hashtag) we can score to what extent the classifier trained a model of the emotion in tweets successfully.

Note that hashtags that add a specific emotion to otherwise unemotional tweets are good indicators themselves for detecting emotion in Twitter. Our goal, however, is to create generalizable models of emotion in Twitter that are not restricted to the occurrence of a hashtag.

4 Experimental setup

4.1 Data collection

As a starting point of our experiments we selected 24 hashtags used in Dutch tweets. The selection was inspired on a list of the 2,500 most frequent hashtags in 2011 and 2012, generated from `twiqs.nl`, a database of Dutch tweets from December 2010 onwards (Tjong Kim Sang and van den Bosch, 2013). Typically, emotion hashtags are not linked to any specific point in time, and therefore surface in such a list generated from an extended period of tweets.

To create the training data, tweets containing any of the hashtags were collected through `twiqs.nl` from the time frame of December 2010 up and until January 2013.

We queried a large sample of Dutch tweets (3,144,781) posted on February 1st 2013, a small portion of which was used as negative examples for our training data, and the rest was used as test data.

4.2 Classification

For each of the hashtags, training data was generated by balancing the amount of collected tweets containing the hashtag with an equal amount of randomly selected tweets (not containing the hashtag) drawn from the set of tweets collected on February 1st, 2013. The resulting binary classifier was tested on the remainder of tweets in this set.

The tweets were pre-processed by extracting word unigrams, bigrams, and trigrams as features. We maintained capitalization and included punctuation and emoticons as tokens in the n-grams, as we expected such tokens to have predictive power in the context of emotions. Both usernames and URLs were normalized to dummy values. All features containing a target hashtag were removed.

Classification was performed by the Balanced Winnow algorithm (Littlestone, 1988). This algorithm is known to offer state-of-the-art results in text classification, and produces interpretable per-class weights that can be used to, for example, inspect the highest-ranking features for one class label. The α and β parameters were set to 1,05 and 0,95 respectively. The major threshold ($\theta+$) and the minor threshold ($\theta-$) were set to 2,5 and 0,5. The number of iterations was bounded to a maximum of three.

4.3 Evaluation

Performance was evaluated by classifying all test tweets and counting the number of tweets with the target hashtag that were positively classified as such, deriving a true positive rate (recall), false positive rate, and area under the curve (AUC) score (Fawcett, 2004).

While this first evaluation gives an indication of the predictability of any hashtag, the ultimate value of a hashtag for emotion detection can be scored by assessing the emotion in positively classified tweets that do not contain the hashtag. This is done by manually annotating the fraction of these tweets that are most confidently positively ranked by the hashtag classifier, as containing the emotion signalled by the hashtag. Three annotators inspected the top-250 of these rankings.

5 Results

5.1 Hashtag predictability

The results of our classifiers labeling a large sample of tweets posted on February 1, 2013 are listed in Table 1. Each line with a target hashtag represents a separate experiment. The amount of training tweets ranges from 19 thousand to 677 thousand for the target hashtag (balanced by an equal amount of random tweets as negative category). The results are sorted by the AUC score.

In this first evaluation our attention focuses on the tweets that have one of the target hashtags. The hashtags themselves are removed at classification time, as our goal is to measure how well our classifiers are able to detect these 'hidden' tags. In this particular stream of tweets, only a limited number of tweets occur that are labeled with our hashtags; the most frequent tag #zinin ('looking forward to it') occurs 1,328 times. Taking #zinin as example, the #zinin classifier labels 158,429 of the test tweets as likely candidates for the hashtag #zinin. Although this is a substantial overprediction, partly caused by the 50%-50% ratio between positive and negative cases in the training set, this still amounts to a false positive rate of only 6%. More importantly, of the 1,328 cases for which it should have predicted #zinin, the classifier labels 1,186 cases correctly, attaining a true positive rate of 89%. The area under the curve (AUC) in true positive rate–false positive rate space is 91%.

Inspecting the performance for all 24 hashtags we observe that about half of the hashtags obtain an AUC of .80 or more. The influence of the amount of training data on the AUC score seems peripheral. Furthermore, there is no clear difference in the predictability of hashtags denoting a positive or negative emotion. The predominantly negative hashtags #geenzin, #fml, #balen and #nietleuk obtain a high AUC, while the other negative hashtags #grr, #bah and #stom are not as predictable. There does not seem to be an a priori property that makes a hashtag more or less predictable, indicating the need for experimentation to confirm the usefulness of a hashtag for emotion detection.

Interestingly, some pairs of synonymous hashtags (#jippie-#joepie, #wauw–#wow, #yes–#yeah, homophonous variants of the same exclamation) and antonymous hashtags (#zinin–#geenzin, #fml–#lml) achieve similar AUC scores. This outcome supports the validity of our approach. Synonymous and antonymous hashtags are employed in similar contexts and should therefore have a similar predictability. This is indeed confirmed by our results. There are counterexamples, however. The pair #yay–#jeej exhibits dissimilar scores. In the case of #leuk there are two antonyms: #nietleuk and #stom. #leuk and #nietleuk have a dissimilar score, while #leuk and #stom are rather

Target hashtag	Gloss	# Training tweets	Target instances on test day	Instances classified	Instances correct	TPR	FPR	AUC
#zinin	looking forward to it	677,156	1,328	158,429	1,186	0.89	0.06	**0.91**
#geenzin	not looking forward to it	427,602	653	231,463	583	0.89	0.08	**0.91**
#fml	fuck my life	139,044	308	126,045	265	0.86	0.05	**0.90**
#lml	love my life	41,031	197	343,936	167	0.85	0.11	0.87
#balen	bummer	219,342	134	271,308	108	0.81	0.09	0.86
#jeej	yay	107,667	31	353,807	25	0.81	0.12	0.85
#nietleuk	not nice	85,825	43	359,709	33	0.77	0.12	0.83
#yeah	yeah	290,288	328	349,598	247	0.75	0.12	0.82
#loveit	love it	259,935	336	290,822	247	0.74	0.10	0.82
#jippie	yippie	66,992	27	396,805	21	0.78	0.13	0.82
#joepie	yippie	53,217	39	422,348	29	0.74	0.14	0.80
#yes	yes	115,707	151	373,874	104	0.69	0.12	0.78
#yay	yay	50,737	45	421,660	31	0.69	0.14	0.78
#hmm	hmm	110,171	95	341,936	63	0.66	0.11	0.78
#grr	argh	70,659	145	397,201	97	0.67	0.13	0.77
#like	like	68,499	284	412,714	178	0.63	0.13	0.75
#woehoe	woohoo	19,236	32	584,552	22	0.69	0.19	0.75
#leuk	nice	391,626	971	307,277	592	0.61	0.11	0.75
#bah	grose	298,842	228	273,454	127	0.56	0.10	0.73
#stom	lame	72,957	99	355,731	57	0.58	0.12	0.73
#omg	oh my god	590,560	145	394,447	79	0.54	0.13	0.71
#wauw	wow	146,145	103	467,503	58	0.56	0.15	0.70
#wow	wow	52,488	50	587,662	29	0.58	0.19	0.70
#huh	huh	48,456	25	352,396	12	0.48	0.11	0.68

Table 1: Results for the prediction of a target hashtag for about 3,1 million Dutch tweets posted on February 1st 2013 (TPR = True Positive Rate, FPR = False Positive Rate, AUC = Area Under the ROC Curve

similar.

5.2 Emotion detection

The second evaluation is based on the manual annotation of the 250 tweets most positively ranked by a hashtag classifier, on the emotion linked to the target hashtag. Due to the labour-intensive nature of this evaluation, it was not possible to analyze all 24 hashtags. We focused on the output for #zinin, #geenzin, #fml and #omg. The first three achieved the highest true positive rates ranging between 86% and 89%, and AUC scores of 90% to 91%. The latter was included as a comparison, expecting a poor emotion detection in view of its bad predictability.

For these four hashtags the 250 'false positives' of which the classifier was most certain were annotated by the three authors by taking the binary decision whether a tweet conveyes the emotion presumed in tweets containing the hashtag. The emotions most strongly linked to the four hashtags were the following:

- #zinin: conveying anticipatory excitement;
- #geenzin: conveying uneagerness
- #fml: conveying self pity
- #omg: conveying an aroused level of indignation, fear, or excitement

Note that #omg is not linked to a single emotion, but rather strengthens several sorts of emotions. This might have been a hampering factor for its predictability. In the annotation for #omg we focused on all three emotions.

Table 2 displays the precision scores when taking a simple majority decision over the three annotators (67% majority) and when only counting the cases in which all three annotators agreed (100% majority). The outcomes show reasonably high precision levels for #zinin (75%) and #fml (69%) along with equally reasonable mutual F-scores between the annotators (67% for #zinin and 81% for #fml), although Cohen's Kappa is rather low in some cases. On the other hand, #geenzin lags behind with a majority precision of 31%. Also the top 250 for #omg does not often display any of the three most strongly linked emotions.

Plotting the annotations of the ranked tweets in precision-at curves, shown in Figure 1, provides further insight into the emotion detection quality in relation to the confidence ranks. Precisions at higher rank cutoffs tend to peak early (indicating that the first top-ranked tweets fit the hashtag best), and decrease slowly or reach a plateau.

	Precision (67% majority)	Precision (100% majority)	Cohen's Kappa	Mutual F-score
#zinin	.75	.35	.09	.67
#geenzin	.31	.21	.60	.73
#fml	.69	.46	.48	.81
#omg	.49	.25	.29	.67

Table 2: Precision of correct hashtag predictions of the top 250 'false positives' based on human annotations

The twofold evaluation that was employed in this study underlines the difference between hashtag predictability and emotion detection. Regarding the three best performing hashtags in terms of predictability, only two, #zinin and #fml, provide utilizable data for emotion detection. Tweets retrieved based on #geenzin seem to have a less overt relation to the emotion of uneagerness, although other cues (such as topical words indirectly related to the emotion) lead to a fairly correct recovery of tweets that had the hashtag. Comparing the two evaluations for #omg, scoring low on both, we may assume that hashtag predictability is a requirement for a proper emotion detection.

6 Discussion

6.1 Feature categories

While classifier performance gives an indication of its ability to detect emotional tweets per hashtag, the strong indicators of those hashtags discovered by the classifiers may provide additional insight into the usage patterns of emotional hashtags by Twitter users. Having scored the emotion detection quality of four hashtags, we set out to analyze the predictive features of these hashtags. To this end we inspected the feature weights assigned by the Balanced Winnow classifier ranked by the strength of their connection to the emotion label, taking into account the 150 tokens and n-grams with the highest positive weight towards the hashtag.

Based on an analysis of the top 150 features for the four hashtags, we distinguished seven categories of features: other emotion-bearing hashtags, emoticons, exclamations, states of being, time expressions, topic reference, and remaining features. Example features for each category, as well as their share in the top 150 features for each hashtag, are presented in Table 3. The percentages give an impression of the most dominant types of features in the prediction of the hashtags.

A first observation is that the top features of the #geenzin classifier are predominantly topic related; the list hardly contains any feature that bears emotion. This is in line with the poor performance on the emotion detection evaluation, while the high AUC score can be explained by a relative consistency of the hashtag being used with topical words that have an indirect relation with the emotion, such as homework for school. The more accurate classifier for the opposite of #geenzin, #zinin, uses more temporal references pointing to the event the person is looking forward to. Also, Dutch positive adjectives such as 'lekker' ('nice') and 'gezellig' (multiple translations[2]), which are strong predictors for #zinin, add to the accuracy of the classifier. There are no clear counterparts for the emotion linked to the opposing #geenzin.

The percentages for #omg display the largest shares of emotion hashtags, emoticons and exclamations, confirming our impression that #omg functions as an intensifying marker of different emotions; this is also reflected in the high percentage of features in the 'other' category.

The most predictive features for the #fml classifier consist of quite some emoticons, emotional hashtags and exclamations. Furthermore, this classifier contains most features in the 'state of being' category, mostly relating to the complex emotion of self pity.

6.2 Emotional cues in Twitter

In contrast to spoken or face-to-face communication, Twitter does not allow for the use of special intonation or facial expressions to mark a message. However, authors on Twitter have other cues at their disposal. Previous studies show, for example, that they might mark the irony or sarcasm in their message by using linguistic markers such

[2]See http://en.wikipedia.org/wiki/Gezelligheid

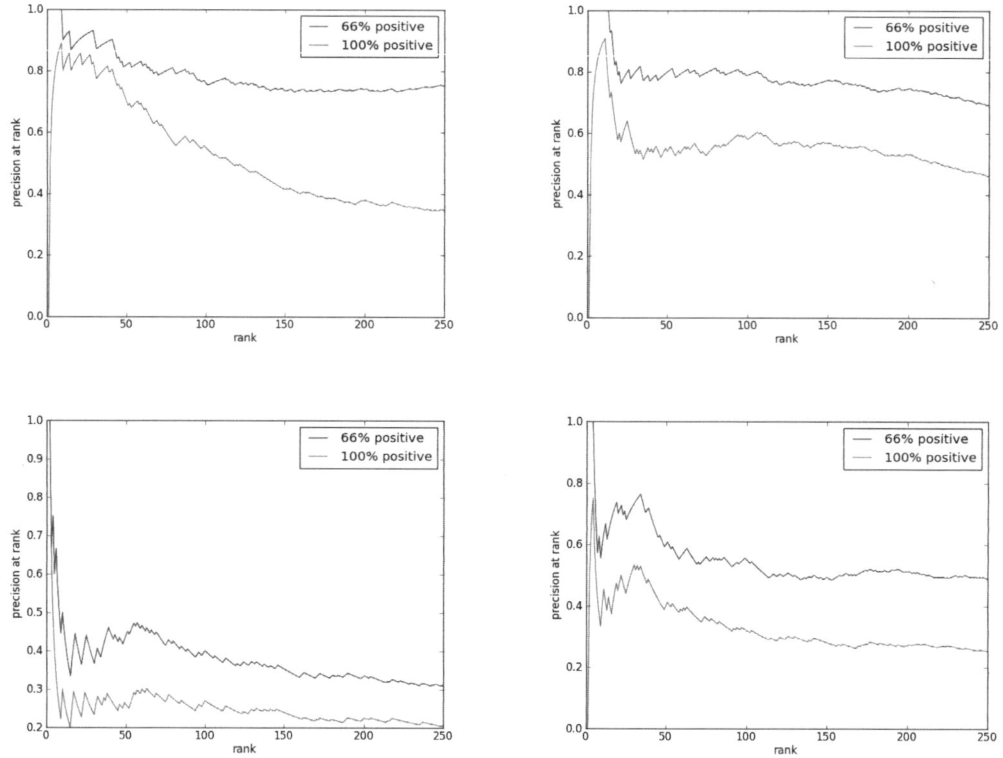

Figure 1: Precision at $\{1 \ldots 250\}$ on the classes #zinin (top left), #fml (top right), #geenzin (bottom left), and #omg (bottom right).

as hyperboles, exclamations and emoticons to help readers to correctly interpret the message (Burgers et al., 2012; Liebrecht et al., 2013). We argue that this is also the case for emotional messages.

Tweets are written messages with a strongly restricted length. Authors compensate the lack of non-verbal cues by adding emotion markers. This hypothesis is supported by research in the field of Computer-Mediated Communication (CMC), where many studies have been carried out on (the lack of) non-verbal emotional cues in (electronic) messages. Walther (1992) introduced the Social Information Processing Perspective: a theory that users can develop relationships via CMC if they have sufficient time and message exchanges and if communicative cues, such as non-verbal emotional cues, are available. He argues that humans easily switch between verbal and non-verbal cues. Based on previous studies, Walther distinguishes textual cues that express affection: relational icons (emoticons, see Asteroff, 1987), electronic paralanguage (such as intentional misspelling (*veeeery*), capitalization (*NICE*), repetition of exclamation marks (*good!!!!!*) and lexical surrogates for vocal segregates (*hmmm*) (Carey, 1980). Later he also recognizes emoticons as nonverbal emotion cues (Walther and D'Addario, 2001). Emoticons can serve many purposes, one of which is expressing emotions (Agarwal et al., 2011; Davidov et al., 2010).

7 Conclusion

In our experiments we showed that machine learning classifiers can be relatively successful both in predicting the hashtag with tweets which were indeed tagged with them, and classifying tweets without the hashtag as exhibiting the emotion denoted by the hashtag, for two of the four fully analysed hashtags: #zinin and #fml. In contrast, the classifier of the hashtag #geenzin was only able to re-link tweets that are stripped from the target hashtag with this hashtag, but failed to capture the complex emotion behind the hashtag. The performance of the #omg classifier lags behind in both tasks.

These findings can be explained by the assumption we made that in order to be a proper emotion label, the context of the hashtag (the rest of the

	Example	Percentage in top 150 features			
		#zinin	#fml	#geenzin	#omg
emotion hashtag	'#foreveralone'	6.67%	10.00%	2.67%	18.67%
emoticon	':S'	0.00%	4.67%	0.00%	6.67%
exclamation	'noooo'	0.00%	2.67%	0.00%	8.67%
state of being	'curious'	3.33%	7.33%	3.33%	0.67%
temporal reference	'moment'	26.00%	7.33%	10.00%	1.33%
topic	'dentist'	52.67%	48.67%	69.33%	25.33%
other	'ready_to'	11.33%	19.33%	14.67%	38.67%

Table 3: Shares (in percentages) of seven categories in the top-150 highest-weighted features for four hashtags.

tweet) would need to convey the same emotion as the hashtag. This appears to be the case with #zinin and #fml. We may assume that the message in tweets with #zinin or #fml carries the emotion itself, which is intensified by the hashtag. The alternative relation between the hashtag and the text is that a hashtag adds emotion to an otherwise neutral message: a signalling function. It seems that most of the tweets tagged with #geenzin are examples of this second relation. The classifier performed well at the re-link task, indicating that it was able to exploit the consistent use of predictive words and phrases, but less well as an emotion detector when we applied the classifier to unseen tweets that do not carry the hashtag. The topical words the classifier used as predictive features appear to be used in several other settings in which no emotion is conveyed, or different emotions than the one expressed by #geenzin. The fourth hashtag that was fully analysed, #omg, turned out to be overall difficult for our classifier. We defined #omg as conveying an aroused level of indignation, fear or excitement. In comparison to the other three hashtags, this definition is less strictly linked to one emotion (Kim et al., 2012). Rather, the hashtag is used in the context of three different emotions and is in itself not an emotion, but an emotion intensifier. Possibly, as a result thereof the tweets are more diverse and the hashtag #omg occurs more frequently with other linguistic elements to express emotion, such as emotional hashtags, emoticons and exclamations.

Although time restrictions prevented us from performing a similar analysis of more hashtags, we can conclude that hashtag predictability is fairly high for most of the 24 hashtags in our set. Interestingly, a considerate part of the synonymous and antonymous hashtags led to similar scores, indicating a relationship between the type of emotion conveyed by a hashtag and the degree of consistency by which the hashtag is employed by users. Whether the degree of consistency, along with an intensifying or emotion adding deployment, can be deduced from the inherent properties of an emotion hashtag is open for future research.

Acknowledgments

This research was supported by the Dutch national program COMMIT as part of the Infiniti project.

References

Apoorv Agarwal, Boyi Xie, Ilia Vovsha, Owen Rambow, and Rebecca Passonneau. 2011. Sentiment analysis of twitter data. In *Proceedings of the Workshop on Languages in Social Media*, pages 30–38. Association for Computational Linguistics.

Cecilia Ovesdotter Alm, Dan Roth, and Richard Sproat. 2005. Emotions from text: machine learning for text-based emotion prediction. In *Proceedings of the Conference on Human Language Technology and Empirical Methods in Natural Language Processing*, pages 579–586. Association for Computational Linguistics.

Saima Aman and Stan Szpakowicz. 2007. Identifying expressions of emotion in text. In *Text, Speech and Dialogue*, pages 196–205. Springer.

Christian Burgers, Margot van Mulken, and Peter Jan Schellens. 2012. Verbal irony differences in usage across written genres. *Journal of Language and Social Psychology*, 31(3):290–310.

John Carey. 1980. Paralanguage in computer mediated communication. In *Proceedings of the 18th annual meeting on Association for Computational Linguistics*, pages 67–69. Association for Computational Linguistics.

Stephen Dann. 2010. Twitter content classification. *First Monday*, 15(12).

Dmitry Davidov, Oren Tsur, and Ari Rappoport. 2010. Enhanced sentiment learning using twitter hashtags and smileys. In *Proceedings of the 23rd International Conference on Computational Linguistics: Posters*, pages 241–249. Association for Computational Linguistics.

Paul Ekman. 1971. Universals and cultural differences in facial expressions of emotion. In *Nebraska symposium on motivation*. University of Nebraska Press.

T. Fawcett. 2004. ROC graphs: Notes and practical considerations for researchers. Technical Report HPL-2003-4, Hewlett Packard Labs.

Alec Go, Richa Bhayani, and Lei Huang. 2009. Twitter sentiment classification using distant supervision. *CS224N Project Report, Stanford*, pages 1–12.

Roberto González-Ibáñez, Smaranda Muresan, and Nina Wacholder. 2011. Identifying sarcasm in twitter: A closer look. In *Proceedings of the 49th Annual Meeting of the Association for Computational Linguistics: Human Language Technologies*, pages 581–586.

Jeff Huang, Katherine M Thornton, and Efthimis N Efthimiadis. 2010. Conversational tagging in twitter. In *Proceedings of the 21st ACM conference on Hypertext and hypermedia*, pages 173–178. ACM.

Sepandar D Kamvar and Jonathan Harris. 2011. We feel fine and searching the emotional web. In *Proceedings of the fourth ACM international conference on Web search and data mining*, pages 117–126. ACM.

Suin Kim, JinYeong Bak, and Alice Haeyun Oh. 2012. Do you feel what i feel? social aspects of emotions in twitter conversations. In *ICWSM*.

Christine Liebrecht, Florian Kunneman, and Antal Van den Bosch. 2013. The perfect solution for detecting sarcasm in tweets #not. In *Proceedings of the 4th Workshop on Computational Approaches to Subjectivity, Sentiment and Social Media Analysis*, pages 29–37, Atlanta, Georgia, June. Association for Computational Linguistics.

N. Littlestone. 1988. Learning quickly when irrelevant attributes abound: A new linear-threshold algorithm. *Machine Learning*, 2:285–318.

Mike Mintz, Steven Bills, Rion Snow, and Dan Jurafsky. 2009. Distant supervision for relation extraction without labeled data. In *Proceedings of the Joint Conference of the 47th Annual Meeting of the ACL and the 4th International Joint Conference on Natural Language Processing of the AFNLP: Volume 2-Volume 2*, pages 1003–1011. Association for Computational Linguistics.

Saif M Mohammad. 2012. #emotional tweets. In *Proceedings of the First Joint Conference on Lexical and Computational Semantics-Volume 1: Proceedings of the main conference and the shared task, and Volume 2: Proceedings of the Sixth International Workshop on Semantic Evaluation*, pages 246–255. Association for Computational Linguistics.

Alexander Pak and Patrick Paroubek. 2010. Twitter as a corpus for sentiment analysis and opinion mining. In *LREC*.

Robert Plutchik. 1980. *Emotion: A psychoevolutionary synthesis*. Harper & Row New York.

Matthew Purver and Stuart Battersby. 2012. Experimenting with distant supervision for emotion classification. In *Proceedings of the 13th Conference of the European Chapter of the Association for Computational Linguistics*, pages 482–491. Association for Computational Linguistics.

Ashequl Qadir and Ellen Riloff. 2013. Bootstrapped learning of emotion hashtags# hashtags4you. In *WASSA 2013*, page 2.

Alan Ritter, Colin Cherry, and Bill Dolan. 2010. Unsupervised modeling of twitter conversations. In *Human Language Technologies: The 2010 Annual Conference of the North American Chapter of the Association for Computational Linguistics*, HLT '10, pages 172–180, Stroudsburg, PA, USA. Association for Computational Linguistics.

Kirk Roberts, Michael A Roach, Joseph Johnson, Josh Guthrie, and Sanda M Harabagiu. 2012. Empatweet: Annotating and detecting emotions on twitter. In *Proceedings of the Eighth International Conference on Language Resources and Evaluation*, pages 3806–3813.

Jared Suttles and Nancy Ide. 2013. Distant supervision for emotion classification with discrete binary values. In *Computational Linguistics and Intelligent Text Processing*, pages 121–136. Springer.

Erik Tjong Kim Sang and Antal van den Bosch. 2013. Dealing with big data: The case of twitter. *Computational Linguistics in the Netherlands Journal*, 3:121–134, 12/2013.

Joseph B Walther and Kyle P D'Addario. 2001. The impacts of emoticons on message interpretation in computer-mediated communication. *Social Science Computer Review*, 19(3):324–347.

Joseph B Walther. 1992. Interpersonal effects in computer-mediated interaction a relational perspective. *Communication research*, 19(1):52–90.

Wenbo Wang, Lu Chen, Krishnaprasad Thirunarayan, and Amit P Sheth. 2012. Harnessing twitter "big data" for automatic emotion identification. In *Privacy, Security, Risk and Trust (PASSAT), 2012 International Conference on and 2012 International Confernece on Social Computing (SocialCom)*, pages 587–592. IEEE.

Finding Arguing Expressions of Divergent Viewpoints in Online Debates

Amine Trabelsi
Department of Computing Science
University of Alberta
atrabels@ualberta.ca

Osmar R. Zaïane
Department of Computing Science
University of Alberta
zaiane@ualberta.ca

Abstract

This work suggests a fine-grained mining of contentious documents, specifically online debates, towards a summarization of contention issues. We propose a Joint Topic Viewpoint model (JTV) for the unsupervised identification and the clustering of arguing expressions according to the latent topics they discuss and the implicit viewpoints they voice. A set of experiments is conducted on online debates documents. Qualitative and quantitative evaluations of the model's output are performed in context of different contention issues. Analysis of experimental results shows the effectiveness of the proposed model to automatically and accurately detect recurrent patterns of arguing expressions in online debate texts.

1 Introduction

This paper addresses the issue of improving the quality of opinion mining from online contentious texts like the posts in debate sites. Mining and summarizing these new resources is crucial, especially when the opinion is related to a subject that stimulates divergent viewpoints within people (e.g. Healthcare Reform, Same-Sex Marriage). We refer to such subjects as issues of contentions. A ***contentious issue*** is "*likely to cause disagreement between people*" (cf. Oxford Dictionaries). Documents such as debate sites' posts may contain multiple contrastive viewpoints regarding a particular issue of contention. Table 1 presents an example of short-text documents expressing divergent opinions where each is exclusively supporting or opposing a healthcare legislation [1].

[1]extracted from a Gallup Inc. survey http://www.gallup.com/poll/126521/favor-oppose-obama-healthcare-plan.aspx

Opinion in contentious issues is often expressed implicitly, not necessarily through the usage of usual negative or positive opinion words, like "bad" or "great". This makes its extraction a challenging task. It is usually conveyed through the arguing expression justifying the endorsement of a particular point of view. The act of arguing is "to give reasons why you think that something is right/wrong, true/not true, etc, especially to persuade people that you are right" (cf. Oxford Dictionaries). For example, the arguing expression "many people do not have healthcare", in Table 1, implicitly explains that the reform is intended to fix the problem of uninsured people, and thus, the opinion is probably on the supporting side. On the other hand, the arguing expression "it will produce too much debt" denotes the negative consequence that may result from passing the bill, making it on the opposing side.

The automatic identification and clustering of these kind of arguing expressions, according to their topics and the viewpoints they convey, is enticing for a variety of application domains. For instance, it can save journalists a substantial amount of work and provide them with drafting elements (viewpoints and associated arguing expressions) about controversial issues. In addition, it would enhance the output quality of the opinion summarization task in general.

The rest of this paper is organized as follows. Section 2 covers the details of the problem statement. Section 3 explains the key issues in the context of recent related work. Section 4 provides the technical details of our model, the Joint Topic Viewpoint model (JTV) . Section 5 describes the clustering task that might be used to obtain a feasible solution. Section 6 provides a description of the experimental set up. Section 7 assesses the adequacy and the performance of our solution. Section 8 concludes the paper.

Support Viewpoint	*Oppose Viewpoint*
Many people do not have health care	The government should not be involved
Provide health care for 30 million people	It will produce too much debt
The government should help old people	The bill would not help the people

Table 1: Excerpts of support and opposition opinion to a healthcare bill in the USA.

2 Problem Statement

This paper examines the task of mining the topics and the viewpoints of arguing expressions towards the summarization of contentious text. An example of a human-made summary of arguing expressions (Jones, 2010) on, what is commonly known as, the Obama healthcare reform is presented in Table 2. Ultimately, the target is to automatically generate similar summaries given a corpus of contentious documents. However, this paper tackles the sub-problem of identifying recurrent words and phrases expressing arguing and cluster them according to their topics and viewpoints. This would help solve the general problem. We use Table 2's examples to define some key concepts which can help us formulate this latter. Here, the contentious issue yielding the divergent positions is the Obama healthcare. The documents are people's verbatim responses to the question "Why do you favor or oppose a healthcare legislation similar to President Obama's ?".

We define a ***contention question*** as a question that can generate expressions of two or more divergent viewpoints as a response.

While the previous question explicitly asks for the reasons ("why"), we relax this constraint and consider also usual opinion questions like "Is the passing of Obamacare bad for Americans ?" or "Do you favor or oppose Obamacare ?".

A ***contentious document*** is a document that contains expressions of one or more divergent viewpoints in response to the contention question. In the context of online debate, a post usually expresses one viewpoint, although it can mention arguing used to justify a different viewpoint.

Table 2 is split into two parts according to the viewpoint: supporting or opposing the healthcare bill. Each row contains one or more phrases, each expressing a reason (or an explanation), e.g. "costs are out of control" and "would help control costs". Though lexically different, these phrases share a common hidden theme (or topic), e.g. insurance's cost, and implicitly convey the same hidden viewpoint's semantics, e.g. support the healthcare bill. Thus, we define an ***arguing expression*** as the set of reasons (words or phrases) sharing a common topic and justifying the same viewpoint regarding a contentious issue.

We assume that a ***viewpoint*** (e.g. a column of Table 2) in a contentious document is a stance, in response to a contention question, which is implicitly expressed by a set of arguing expressions (e.g. rows of a column in Table 2).

Thus, the arguing expressions voicing the same viewpoint differ in their topics, but agree in the stance. For example, arguing expressions represented by "system is broken" and "costs are out of control" discuss different topics, i.e. healthcare system and insurance's cost, but both support the healthcare bill. On the other hand, arguing expressions of divergent viewpoints may have similar topic or may not. For instance, "government should help elderly" and "government should not be involved" share the same topic, i.e. government's role, while conveying opposed viewpoints.

Our research problem and objectives in terms of the newly introduced concepts are stated as follows. Given a corpus of unlabeled contentious documents $\{doc_1, doc_2, .., doc_D\}$, where each document doc_d expresses one or more viewpoints $\vec{v}^d$ from a set of L possible viewpoints $\{v_1, v_2, .., v_L\}$, and each viewpoint v_l can be conveyed using one or more arguing expressions $\vec{\phi}_l$ from a set of possible arguing expressions discussing K different topics $\{\phi_{1l}, \phi_{2l}, .., \phi_{Kl}\}$, the objective is to perform the following two tasks:

1. automatically extracting coherent words and phrases describing any distinct arguing expression ϕ_{kl};

2. grouping extracted distinct arguing expressions ϕ_{kl} for different topics, $k = 1..K$, into their corresponding viewpoint v_l.

This paper focuses on the first task while laying the ground for solving the second one. In carrying out the first task, we must meet the main challenge of recognizing arguing expressions having

Support Viewpoint	*Oppose Viewpoint*
People need health insurance/too many uninsured	Will raise cost of insurance/ less affordable
System is broken/needs to be fixed	Does not address real problems
Costs are out of control/would help control costs	Need more information on how it works
Moral responsibility to provide/Fair	Against big government involvement (general)
Would make healthcare more affordable	Government should not be involved in healthcare
Don't trust insurance companies	Cost the government too much

Table 2: Human-made summary of arguing expressions supporting and opposing Obamacare.

the same topic and viewpoint but which are lexically different, e.g. "provide health care for 30 million people " and " many people do not have healthcare". For this purpose we propose a Joint Topic Viewpoint Model (JTV) to account for the dependence structure of topics and viewpoints.

3 Related Work

3.1 Classifying Stances

An early body of work addresses the challenge of classifying viewpoints in contentious or ideological discourses using supervised techniques (Kim and Hovy, 2007; Lin et al., 2006). Although the models give good performances, they remain data-dependent and costly to label, making the unsupervised approach more appropriate for the existing huge quantity of online data. A similar trend of studies scrutinizes the discourse aspect of a document in order to identify opposed stances (Thomas et al., 2006; Park et al., 2011). However, these methods utilize polarity lexicon to detect opinionated text and do not look for arguing expression, which is shown to be useful in recognizing opposed stances (Somasundaran and Wiebe, 2010). Somasundaran and Wiebe (2010) classify ideological stances in online debates using a generated arguing clues from the Multi Perspective Question Answering (MPQA) opinion corpus[2]. Our problem is not to classify documents, but to recognize recurrent pattern of arguing phrases instead of arguing clues. Moreover, our approach is independent of any annotated corpora.

3.2 Topic Modeling in Reviews Data

Another emerging body of work applies probabilistic topic models on reviews data to extract appraisal aspects and the corresponding specific sentiment lexicon. These kinds of models are usually referred to as joint sentiment/aspect topic models (Jo and Oh, 2011; Titov and McDonald, 2008; Zhao et al., 2010). Lin and He (2009) propose the Joint Sentiment Topic Model (JST) to model the dependency between sentiment and topics. They make the assumption that topics discussed on a review are conditioned on sentiment polarity. Reversely, our JTV model assumes that a viewpoint endorsement (e.g., oppose reform) is conditioned on the discussed topic (e.g., government's role) and its application is different from that of JST. Most of the joint aspect sentiment topic models are either semi-supervised or weakly supervised using sentiment polarity words (Paradigm lists) to boost their efficiency. In our case, viewpoints are often expressed implicitly and finding specific arguing lexicon for different stances is a challenging task in itself. Indeed, our model is enclosed in another body of work that based on a probabilistic Topic Model framework to mine divergent viewpoints.

3.3 Topic Modeling in Contentious Text

A recent study by Mukherjee and Liu (2012) examines mining contention from discussion forums data where the interaction between different authors is pivotal. It attempts to jointly discover contention/agreement indicators (CA-Expressions) and topics using three different Joint Topic Expressions Models (JTE). The JTEs' output is used to discover points (topics) of contention. The model supposes that people express agreement or disagreement through CA-expressions. However, this is not often the case when people express their viewpoint via other channels than discussion forums like debate sites or editorials. Moreover, agreement or disagreement may also be conveyed implicitly through arguing expressions rejecting or supporting another opinion. JTEs do not model viewpoints and use the supervised Maximum Entropy model to detect CA-expressions.

Recently, Gottipati et al. (2013) propose a topic model to infer human interpretable text in the do-

[2]http://mpqa.cs.pitt.edu/

main of issues using Debatepedia[3] as a corpus of evidence. Debatepedia is an online authored encyclopedia to summarize and organize the main arguments of two possible positions. The model takes advantage of the hierarchical structure of arguments in Debatepedia. Our work aims to model unstructured online data, with unrestricted number of positions, in order to, ultimately, output a Debatepedia-like summary.

The closest work to ours is the one presented by Paul et al. (2010). It introduces the problem of contrastive summarization which is very similar to our stated problem in Section 2. They propose the Topic Aspect Model (TAM) and use the output distributions to compute similarities' scores for sentences. Scored sentences are used in a modified Random Walk algorithm to generate the summary. The assumption of TAM is that any word in the document can exclusively belong to a topic (e.g., government), a viewpoint (e.g., good), both (e.g., involvement) or neither (e.g., think). However, according to TAM's generative model, an author would choose his viewpoint and the topic to talk about independently. Our JTV encodes the dependency between topics and viewpoints.

4 Joint Topic Viewpoint Model

Latent Dirichlet Allocation (LDA) (Blei et al., 2003) is one of the most popular topic models used to mine large text data sets. It models a document as a mixture of topics where each topic is a distribution over words. However, it fails to model more complex structures of texts like contention where viewpoints are hidden.

We augment LDA to model a contentious document as a pair of dependent mixtures: a mixture of arguing topics and a mixture of viewpoints for each topic. The assumption is that a document discusses the topics in proportions, (e.g. 80% government's role, 20% insurance's cost). Moreover, as explained in Section 2, each one of these topics can be shared by divergent arguing expressions conveying different viewpoints. We suppose that for each discussed topic in the document, the viewpoints are expressed in proportions. For instance, 70% of the document's text discussing the government's role expresses an opposing viewpoint to the reform while 30% of it conveys a supporting viewpoint. Thus, each term in a document is assigned a pair topic-viewpoint label (e.g.

[3]http://dbp.idebate.org

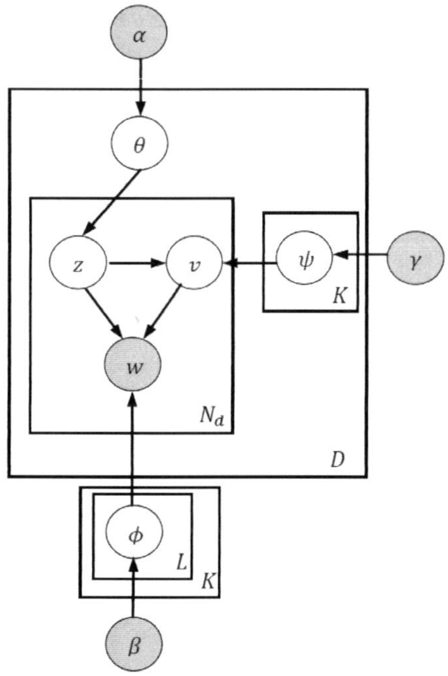

Figure 1: The JTV's graphical model (plate notation)

"government's role-oppose reform"). A term is a word or a phrase i.e. n-grams (n>1). For each topic-viewpoint pair, the model generates a topic-viewpoint probability distribution over terms. This topic-viewpoint distribution would corresponds to what we define as an arguing expression in Section 2, i.e. a set of terms sharing a common topic and justifying the same viewpoint regarding a contentious issue. The Joint Topic Viewpoint (JTV), is similar to the Joint Sentiment Topic model (JST) (Lin and He, 2009), as it models documents as two dependent mixtures. However, here we condition viewpoints on topics instead of conditioning topics on sentiment. Moreover, the application is different from that of JST which intend to model reviews data.

Formally, assume that a corpus contains D documents $d_{1..D}$, where each document is a term's vector $\vec{w}_d$ of size N_d; each term w_{dn} in a document belongs to the corpus vocabulary of distinct terms of size V. Let K be the total number of topics and L be the total number of viewpoints. Let θ_d denote the probabilities (proportions) of K topics under a document d; ψ_{dk} be the probability distributions (proportions) of L viewpoints for a topic k in the document d (the number of viewpoints L is the same for all topics); and ϕ_{kl} be the multinomial probability distribution over terms associated with a topic k and a viewpoint l. The generative process (see. the JTV graphical model in Figure 1) is the following:

- for each topic k and viewpoint l, draw a multinomial distribution over the vocabulary V: $\phi_{kl} \sim Dir(\beta)$;
- for each document d,

  draw a topic mixture $\theta_d \sim Dir(\alpha)$

  for each topic k, draw a viewpoint mixture $\psi_{dk} \sim Dir(\gamma)$

  for each term w_{dn}, sample a topic assignment $z_{dn} \sim Mult(\theta_d)$; sample a viewpoint assignment $v_{dn} \sim Mult(\psi_{dz_{dn}})$; and sample a term $w_{dn} \sim Mult(\phi_{z_{dn}v_{dn}})$.

We use fixed symmetric Dirichlet's parameters γ, β and α. They can be interpreted as the prior counts of: terms assigned to viewpoint l and topic k in a document; a particular term w assigned to topic k and viewpoint l within the corpus; terms assigned to a topic k in a document, respectively.

In order to learn the hidden JTV's parameters ϕ_{kl}, ψ_{dk} and θ_d, we draw on approximate inference as exact inference is intractable (Blei et al., 2003). We use the collapsed Gibbs Sampling (Griffiths and Steyvers, 2004), a Markov Chain Monte Carlo algorithm. The collapsed Gibbs sampler integrate out all parameters ϕ, ψ and θ in the joint distribution of the model and converge to a stationary posterior distribution over viewpoints' assignments $\vec{v}$ and all topics' assignments $\vec{z}$ in the corpus. It iterates on each current observed token w_i and samples each corresponding v_i and z_i given all the previous sampled assignments in the model $\vec{v}_{\neg i}$, $\vec{z}_{\neg i}$ and observed $\vec{w}_{\neg i}$, where $\vec{v} = \{v_i, \vec{v}_{\neg i}\}$, $\vec{z} = \{z_i, \vec{z}_{\neg i}\}$, and $\vec{w} = \{w_i, \vec{w}_{\neg i}\}$. The derived sampling equation is:

$$p(z_i = k, v_i = l | \vec{z}_{\neg i}, \vec{v}_{\neg i}, w_i = t, \vec{w}_{\neg i}) \propto$$
$$\frac{n^{(t)}_{kl,\neg i} + \beta}{\sum_{t=1}^{V} n^{(t)}_{kl,\neg i} + V\beta} \cdot \frac{n^{(l)}_{dk,\neg i} + \gamma}{\sum_{l=1}^{L} n^{(l)}_{dk,\neg i} + L\gamma} . n^{(k)}_{d,\neg i} + \alpha \quad (1)$$

where $n^{(t)}_{kl,\neg i}$ is the number of times term t was assigned to topic k and the viewpoint l in the corpus; $n^{(l)}_{dk,\neg i}$ is the number of times viewpoint l of topic k was observed in document d; and $n^{(k)}_{d,\neg i}$ is the number of times topic k was observed in document d. All these counts are computed excluding the current token i, which is indicated by the symbol $\neg i$.

	AW		GM		ObCare	
View pt	allow	not	illegal	not	bad	not
#doc	213	136	44	54	129	54
tot.#toks	44482		10666		22733	
avg.#toks. doc.	127.45		108.83		124.22	

Table 3: Statistics on the three used data sets

After the convergence of the Gibbs algorithm, the parameters ϕ, ψ and θ are estimated using the last obtained sample.

5 Clustering Arguing Expressions

Although we are not tackling the task of clustering arguing expressions according to their viewpoints in this paper (Task 2 in Section 2), we explain how the structure of JTV lays the ground for performing it. We mentioned in the previous Section that an inferred topic-viewpoint distribution ϕ_{kl} can be assimilated to an arguing expression. For convenience, we will use "arguing expression" and "topic-viewpoint" interchangeably to refer to the topic-viewpoint distribution.

Indeed, two topic-viewpoint ϕ_{kl} and $\phi_{k'l}$, having different topics k and k', do not necessarily express the same viewpoint, despite the fact that they both have the same index l. The reason stems from the nested structure of the model, where the generation of the viewpoint assignments for a particular topic k is completely independent from that of topic k'. In other words, the model does not trace and match the viewpoint labeling along different topics. Nevertheless, the JTV can still help overcome this problem. According to the JTV's structure, a topic-viewpoint ϕ_{kl}, is more similar in distribution to a divergent topic-viewpoint $\phi_{kl'}$, related to the same topic k, than to any other topic-viewpoint $\phi_{k'*}$, corresponding to a different topic k'. Therefore, we can formulate the problem of clustering arguments as a constrained clustering problem (Basu et al., 2008). The goal is to group the similar topics-viewpoints ϕ_{kl}s into L clusters (number of viewpoints), given the constraint that the ϕ_{kl}s of the same topic k should not belong to the same cluster. The similarity between the topic-viewpoint distributions can be measured using the Jensen-Shannon Divergence (Bishop, 2006).

6 Experimental Set up

In order to evaluate the performances of the JTV model, we experiment with three different corpora of contentious documents. Recall, we assume that any input document to the JTV is answering a contentious question which makes it contentious according to the definitions stated in Section 2. Posts in online debate websites, like "createdebate.com" or "debate.org", match this requirement. They correspond to online users' takes on a clearly stated contention question making them more adequate for our matter than debate forums' posts. These latter contain online interactions between users where the objective is not necessarily answering a contention question but rather discussing a contentious topic. Classifying a document as contentious or not is not an issue considered in this paper but can be explored in our future work. Table 3 describes the used data sets.

Assault Weapons (AW) [4]: includes posts extracted from "debate.com". The contention question is "Should assault weapons be allowed in the United States as means of allowing individuals to defend themselves?". The viewpoints are either "should be allowed" or "should not be allowed".

Gay Marriage (GM) [5]: contains posts from "debate.com" related to the contention question "Should gay marriage be illegal?". The posts' stance are either "should be illegal" or "should be legal".

Obama Healthcare (ObCare) [6]: includes posts from "debate.org" responding to the contention question "Is the passing of ObamaCare bad for the American public?". Stances are either "bad" or "not bad".

Paul et al. (2010) stress out the importance of negation features in detecting contrastive viewpoints. Thus, we performed a simple treatment of merging any negation indicators, like "nothing", "no one", "never", etc., found in text with the following occurring word to form a single token. Moreover, we merge the negation "not" with any Auxiliary verb (e.g., is, was, could, will) preceding it. Then, we removed the stop-words.

[4]http://www.debate.org/opinions/should-assault-weapons-be-allowed-in-the-united-states-as-means-of-allowing-individuals-to-defend-themselves

[5]http://www.debate.org/opinions/should-gay-marriage-be-illegal

[6]http://www.debate.org/opinions/is-the-passing-of-obamacare-bad-for-the-american-public

Throughout the experiments below, the JTV's hyperparameters are set to fixed values. The γ is set, according to Steyvers and Griffiths's (Steyvers and Griffiths, 2007) hyperparameters settings, to $50/L$, where L is the number of viewpoints. β and α are adjusted manually, to give reasonable results, and are both set to 0.01. Along the experiments, we try different number of topics K. The number of viewpoints L is equal to 2. The TAM model (Paul et al., 2010) (Section 3.3) is run as a means of comparison during the evaluation procedure. Its default parameters are used.

7 Model Evaluation

7.1 Qualitative Evaluation

Tables 4 and 5 present the inferred topic-viewpoints words, i.e. arguing expressions, by JTV for the Obama Healthcare and Gay Marriage data sets, respectively. We set a number of topics of $K = 3$ for the former and $K = 2$ for the latter. The number of viewpoints is $L = 2$ for both data sets. For the Obamacare data set, we run the model with balanced number of posts from "bad" and "not bad" stances. Each topic-viewpoint pair (e.g. Topic 1-view 1) is represented by the set of top terms. The terms are sorted in descending order according to their probabilities. Inferred probabilities over topics, and over viewpoints for each topic, are also reported. We try to qualitatively observe the distinctiveness of each arguing (topic-viewpoint) and assess the coherence in terms of the topic discussed and the viewpoint conveyed and its divergence with the corresponding pair-element.

In both Tables 4 and 5, most of the topic-viewpoint pairs, corresponding to a same topic, are conveying opposite stances. For instance, taking a closer look to the original data suggests that Topic3-view5 (Table 4) criticizes the healthcare system and compares it to the other countries (e.g. a sample from the original documents:"*revise our* ***healthcare system*** *with the most efficient systems in the* ***world***"). On the other side, Topic 3-view 6 explains the negative consequence of obamacare on middle class, e.g. "***ObamaCare*** *was supposed to help the poor and the* ***middle class***. *In the end, the businesses fire all the people because of the ObamaCare* ***taxes*** *and then IT IS THE* ***MIDDLE CLASS*** *PEOPLE WHO SUFFER!*". Similarly, Topic1-view1 advances the question of the costs that the bill will cause at the level of people

Topic 1	*0.328*	*Topic 2*	*0.334*	*Topic 3*	*0.337*
view 1 *0.64*	*view 2* *0.36*	*view 3* *0.59*	*view 4* *0.41*	*view 5* *0.63*	*view 6* *0.37*
pay	universal	people	insurance	healthcare	obamacare
people	care	insurance	health	obamacare	healthcare
make	life	good	companies	system	government
money	law	free	medicare	americans	class
costs	act	health	doctors	affordable	taxes
government	poor	work	plan	country/world	middle

Table 4: JTV's generated topics-viewpoints (arguing expressions) from Obamacare data set

Topic 1	*0.50*	*Topic 2*	0.50
view 1 *0.47*	*view 2* 0.53	*view 3* *0.60*	*view 4* 0.40
marriage	marriage	people	gay
love	man	gay	children
life	woman	religion	people
couples	god	shouldnt	sex
person	bible	wrong	parents
legal	illegal	rights	natural
married	wrong	government	human
happy	love	marry	population
samesex	homosexual	freedom	opposite
illegal	word	argument	race

Table 5: JTV's generated topics-viewpoints (arguing expressions) from Gay Marriage data set

and government, e.g. *"The **government** doesn't even have enough **money** to **pay** of a fraction of the towering debt that we've accrued*", "forcing **people** to buy insurance or **pay** an even higher tax will **make** more families poverty stricken". However, Topic1-view2 stresses out the importance of having a universal healthcare, e.g. *"ObamaCare certainly has problems, but just like any **law**, we can work on these problems and make the **law** better (..). The fundamental goal is **Universal** Healthcare (...)*", *"If you were **poor** and had a hernia that needed surgery, you need money to pay for it. Denying Obama's Plan for a health **care** system means you cannot pay for it which means you will DIE.*". Similar pattern is observed in Topic 2.

The results on Gay Marriage 1 dataset (Table 5) encompass the notion of shared topic between divergent arguing expressions (Section 2) more clearly than the results obtained from Obamacare. This may be related to the nature of the contention. For instance, Topic 1 in Table 5 is "the concept of marriage" and it is shared by both view 1 and view 2. However, the concept is perceived differently according to the stance. The terms in view 1 (not illegal) suggest that **marriage** is about **love**, **happiness** and it wouldn't disturb anyone's **life** (as it may be read from original data). The view 2 (illegal) may emphasize the notion of a **marriage** as a union between **man** and **woman** and the sacredness aspect of it (**god**, **bible**). Similarly, Topic 2 is about "**people** who are **gay**". The terms in view 3 (not illegal) may advocate that **religious arguments** from opposing stance do not make sense and that **gay people** are **free** and have the same **rights** as other people. Moreover, the **government** should not interfere in this matter. View 4 (illegal) suggests that **gay people** can not have **children** which raises the problem of **population** decrease. It also casts doubt on their ability to be **parents**.

7.2 Quantitative Evaluation

We assess the ability of the model to fit the online debate data and generate distinct topic-viewpoint pairs by comparing it with TAM which models also the topic-viewpoint dimension.

7.2.1 Held-Out Perplexity

We use the perplexity criterion to measure the ability of the learned topic model to fit a new held-out data. Perplexity assesses the generalization performance and, subsequently, provides a com-

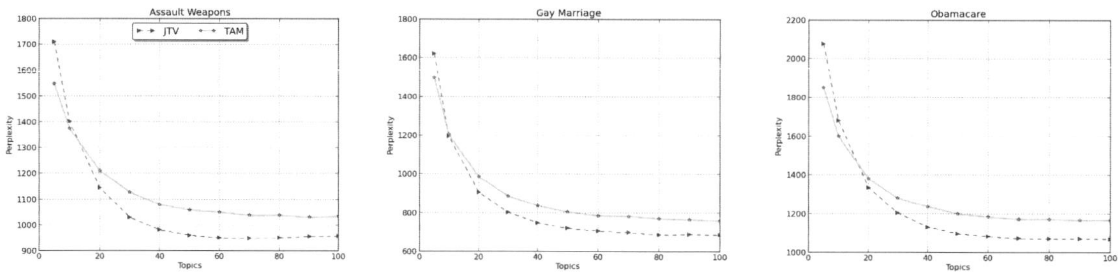

(a) AW (b) GM (c) ObCare

Figure 2: JVT and TAM's perplexity plots for three different data sets

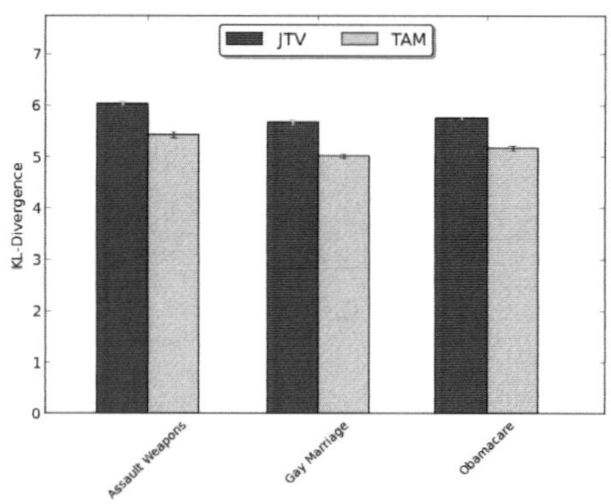

Figure 3: Average of overall topic-viewpoint divergences of JTV and TAM

paring framework of learned topic models. The lower the perplexity, the less "perplexed" is the model by unseen data and the better the generalization. It algebraically corresponds to the inverse geometrical mean of the test corpus' terms likelihoods given the learned model parameters (Heinrich, 2009). We compute the perplexity under estimated parameters of JTV and compare it to that of TAM for our three unigrams data sets (Section 6).

Figure 2 exhibits, for each corpus, the perplexity plot as function of the number of topics K for JTV and TAM. Note that for each K, we run the model 50 times. The drawn perplexity corresponds to the average perplexity on the 50 runs where each run compute one-fold perplexity from a 10-fold cross-validation. The figures show evidence that the JTV outperforms TAM for all data sets, used in the experimentation.

7.2.2 Kullback-Leibler Divergence

Kullback-Leibler (KL) Divergence is used to measure the degree of separation between two probability distributions. We utilize it to assess the distinctiveness of generated topic-viewpoint by JTV and TAM. This is an indicator of a good aggregation of arguing expressions. We compute an overall-divergence quantity, which is an average KL-Divergence between all pairs of topic-viewpoint distributions, for JTV and TAM and compare them. Figure 3 illustrates the results for all datasets. Quantities are averages on 20 runs of the models. Both models are run with a number of topics $K = 5$. Comparing JTV and TAM, we notice that the overall-divergence of JTV's topic-viewpoint is significantly ($p - value < 0.01$) higher for all data sets. This result reveals a better quality of our JTV extracting process of arguing expressions (the first task stated in Section 2)

8 Conclusion

We suggested a fine grained probabilistic framework for improving the quality of opinion mining from online contention texts. We proposed a Joint Topic Viewpoint model (JTV) for the unsupervised detection of arguing expressions. Unlike common approaches the proposed model focuses on arguing expressions that are implicitly described in unstructured text according to the latent topics they discuss and the implicit viewpoints they voice. The qualitative and quantitative analysis of the experimental results show the effectiveness of our (JTV) model in generating informative summaries of recurrent topics and viewpoints patterns in online debates' texts. Future study needs to give more insights into the clustering of arguing expressions according to their viewpoints, as well as their automatic extractive summary.

References

Sugato Basu, Ian Davidson, and Kiri Wagstaff. 2008. *Constrained Clustering: Advances in Algorithms,*

Theory, and Applications. Chapman & Hall/CRC, 1 edition.

Christopher M. Bishop. 2006. *Pattern Recognition and Machine Learning (Information Science and Statistics)*. Springer-Verlag New York, Inc., Secaucus, NJ, USA.

David M. Blei, Andrew Y. Ng, and Michael I. Jordan. 2003. Latent dirichlet allocation. *Journal of Machine Learning Research*, 3:993–1022, March.

Yi Fang, Luo Si, Naveen Somasundaram, and Zhengtao Yu. 2012. Mining contrastive opinions on political texts using cross-perspective topic model. In *Proceedings of the fifth ACM international conference on Web search and data mining*, WSDM '12, pages 63–72, New York, NY, USA. ACM.

Swapna Gottipati, Minghui Qiu, Yanchuan Sim, Jing Jiang, and Noah A. Smith. 2013. Learning topics and positions from debatepedia. In *Proceedings of Conference on Empirical Methods in Natural Language Processing*, EMNLP '13.

Thomas L. Griffiths and Mark Steyvers. 2004. Finding scientific topics. *Proceedings of the National Academy of Sciences of the United States of America*, 101(Suppl 1):5228–5235.

Gregor Heinrich. 2009. Parameter estimation for text analysis. Technical report, Fraunhofer IGD, September.

Yohan Jo and Alice H. Oh. 2011. Aspect and sentiment unification model for online review analysis. In *Proceedings of the fourth ACM international conference on Web search and data mining*, WSDM '11, pages 815–824, New York, NY, USA. ACM.

Jeffrey M. Jones. 2010. In u.s., 45% favor, 48% oppose obama healthcare plan. *Gallup*, March.

Soo-Min Kim and Eduard H Hovy. 2007. Crystal: Analyzing predictive opinions on the web. In *EMNLP-CoNLL*, pages 1056–1064.

Chenghua Lin and Yulan He. 2009. Joint sentiment/topic model for sentiment analysis. In *Proceedings of the 18th ACM conference on Information and knowledge management*, CIKM '09, pages 375–384, New York, NY, USA. ACM.

Wei-Hao Lin, Theresa Wilson, Janyce Wiebe, and Alexander Hauptmann. 2006. Which side are you on?: identifying perspectives at the document and sentence levels. In *Proceedings of the Tenth Conference on Computational Natural Language Learning*, CoNLL-X '06, pages 109–116, Stroudsburg, PA, USA. Association for Computational Linguistics.

Arjun Mukherjee and Bing Liu. 2012. Mining contentions from discussions and debates. In *Proceedings of the 18th ACM SIGKDD international conference on Knowledge discovery and data mining*, KDD '12, pages 841–849, New York, NY, USA. ACM.

Souneil Park, KyungSoon Lee, and Junehwa Song. 2011. Contrasting opposing views of news articles on contentious issues. In *Proceedings of the 49th Annual Meeting of the Association for Computational Linguistics: Human Language Technologies - Volume 1*, HLT '11, pages 340–349, Stroudsburg, PA, USA. Association for Computational Linguistics.

Michael J. Paul, ChengXiang Zhai, and Roxana Girju. 2010. Summarizing contrastive viewpoints in opinionated text. In *Proceedings of the 2010 Conference on Empirical Methods in Natural Language Processing*, EMNLP '10, pages 66–76, Stroudsburg, PA, USA. Association for Computational Linguistics.

Swapna Somasundaran and Janyce Wiebe. 2010. Recognizing stances in ideological on-line debates. In *Proceedings of the NAACL HLT 2010 Workshop on Computational Approaches to Analysis and Generation of Emotion in Text*, CAAGET '10, pages 116–124, Stroudsburg, PA, USA. Association for Computational Linguistics.

Mark Steyvers and Tom Griffiths. 2007. Probabilistic topic models. *Handbook of latent semantic analysis*, 427(7):424–440.

Matt Thomas, Bo Pang, and Lillian Lee. 2006. Get out the vote: determining support or opposition from congressional floor-debate transcripts. In *Proceedings of the 2006 Conference on Empirical Methods in Natural Language Processing*, EMNLP '06, pages 327–335, Stroudsburg, PA, USA. Association for Computational Linguistics.

Ivan Titov and Ryan McDonald. 2008. Modeling online reviews with multi-grain topic models. In *Proceedings of the 17th international conference on World Wide Web*, WWW '08, pages 111–120, New York, NY, USA. ACM.

Wayne Xin Zhao, Jing Jiang, Hongfei Yan, and Xiaoming Li. 2010. Jointly modeling aspects and opinions with a maxent-lda hybrid. In *Proceedings of the 2010 Conference on Empirical Methods in Natural Language Processing*, EMNLP '10, pages 56–65, Stroudsburg, PA, USA. Association for Computational Linguistics.

Aspect Term Extraction for Sentiment Analysis: New Datasets, New Evaluation Measures and an Improved Unsupervised Method

John Pavlopoulos and **Ion Androutsopoulos**
Dept. of Informatics, Athens University of Economics and Business, Greece
http://nlp.cs.aueb.gr/

Abstract

Given a set of texts discussing a particular entity (e.g., customer reviews of a smartphone), aspect based sentiment analysis (ABSA) identifies prominent aspects of the entity (e.g., battery, screen) and an average sentiment score per aspect. We focus on aspect term extraction (ATE), one of the core processing stages of ABSA that extracts terms naming aspects. We make publicly available three new ATE datasets, arguing that they are better than previously available ones. We also introduce new evaluation measures for ATE, again arguing that they are better than previously used ones. Finally, we show how a popular unsupervised ATE method can be improved by using continuous space vector representations of words and phrases.

1 Introduction

Before buying a product or service, consumers often search the Web for expert reviews, but increasingly also for opinions of other consumers, expressed in blogs, social networks etc. Many useful opinions are expressed in text-only form (e.g., in tweets). It is then desirable to *extract aspects* (e.g., screen, battery) from the texts that discuss a particular entity (e.g., a smartphone), i.e., figure out what is being discussed, and also *estimate aspect sentiment scores*, i.e., how positive or negative the (usually average) sentiment for each aspect is. These two goals are jointly known as *Aspect Based Sentiment Analysis* (ABSA) (Liu, 2012).

In this paper, we consider free text customer reviews of products and services; ABSA, however, is also applicable to texts about other kinds of entities (e.g., politicians, organizations). We assume that a search engine retrieves customer reviews about a particular *target entity* (product or service), that multiple reviews written by different customers are retrieved for each target entity, and that the ultimate goal is to produce a table like the one of Fig. 1, which presents the most prominent aspects and average aspect sentiment scores of the target entity. Most ABSA systems in effect perform all or some of the following three subtasks:

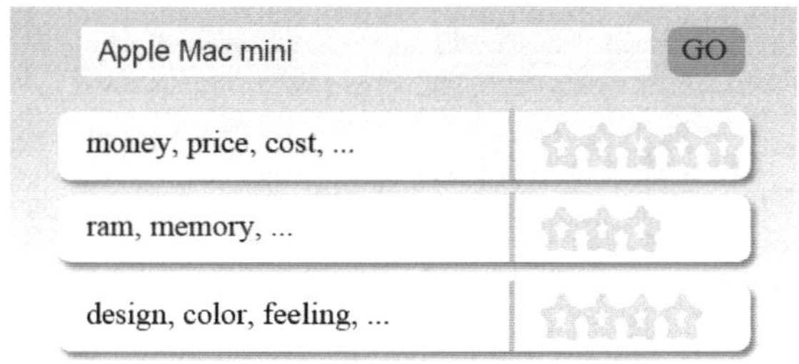

Figure 1: Automatically extracted prominent aspects (shown as clusters of aspect terms) and average aspect sentiment scores of a target entity.

Aspect term extraction: Starting from texts about a particular target entity or entities of the same type as the target entity (e.g., laptop reviews), this stage extracts and possibly ranks by importance *aspect terms*, i.e., terms naming aspects (e.g., 'battery', 'screen') of the target entity, including multi-word terms (e.g., 'hard disk') (Liu, 2012; Long et al., 2010; Snyder and Barzilay, 2007; Yu et al., 2011). At the end of this stage, each aspect term is taken to be the name of a different aspect, but aspect terms may subsequently be clustered during aspect aggregation; see below.

Aspect term sentiment estimation: This stage estimates the polarity and possibly also the intensity (e.g., strongly negative, mildly positive) of the opinions for each aspect term of the target entity, usually averaged over several texts. Classifying texts by sentiment polarity is a popular research topic (Liu, 2012; Pang and Lee, 2005; Tsytsarau and Palpanas, 2012). The goal, however, in this

ABSA subtask is to estimate the (usually average) polarity and intensity of the opinions about particular aspect terms of the target entity.

Aspect aggregation: Some systems group aspect terms that are synonyms or near-synonyms (e.g., 'price', 'cost') or, more generally, cluster aspect terms to obtain aspects of a coarser granularity (e.g., 'chicken', 'steak', and 'fish' may all be replaced by 'food') (Liu, 2012; Long et al., 2010; Zhai et al., 2010; Zhai et al., 2011). A polarity (and intensity) score can then be computed for each coarser aspect (e.g., 'food') by combining (e.g., averaging) the polarity scores of the aspect terms that belong in the coarser aspect.

In this paper, we focus on aspect term extraction (ATE). Our contribution is threefold. Firstly, we argue (Section 2) that previous ATE datasets are not entirely satisfactory, mostly because they contain reviews from a particular domain only (e.g., consumer electronics), or they contain reviews for very few target entities, or they do not contain annotations for aspect terms. We constructed and make publicly available three new ATE datasets with customer reviews for a much larger number of target entities from three domains (restaurants, laptops, hotels), with gold annotations of all the aspect term occurrences; we also measured inter-annotator agreement, unlike previous datasets.

Secondly, we argue (Section 3) that commonly used evaluation measures are also not entirely satisfactory. For example, when precision, recall, and F-measure are computed over *distinct* aspect terms (types), equal weight is assigned to more and less frequent aspect terms, whereas frequently discussed aspect terms are more important; and when precision, recall, and F-measure are computed over aspect term *occurrences* (tokens), methods that identify very few, but very frequent aspect terms may appear to perform much better than they actually do. We propose weighted variants of precision and recall, which take into account the *rankings* of the distinct aspect terms that are obtained when the distinct aspect terms are ordered by their true and predicted frequencies. We also compute the average weighted precision over several weighted recall levels.

Thirdly, we show (Section 4) how the popular *unsupervised* ATE method of Hu and Liu (2004), can be extended with continuous space word vectors (Mikolov et al., 2013a; Mikolov et al., 2013b; Mikolov et al., 2013c). Using our datasets and evaluation measures, we demonstrate (Section 5) that the extended method performs better.

2 Datasets

We first discuss previous datasets that have been used for ATE, and we then introduce our own.

2.1 Previous datasets

So far, ATE methods have been evaluated mainly on customer reviews, often from the consumer electronics domain (Hu and Liu, 2004; Popescu and Etzioni, 2005; Ding et al., 2008).

The most commonly used dataset is that of Hu and Liu (2004), which contains reviews of only five particular electronic products (e.g., Nikon Coolpix 4300). Each sentence is annotated with aspect terms, but inter-annotator agreement has not been reported.[1] All the sentences appear to have been selected to express clear positive or negative opinions. There are no sentences expressing conflicting opinions about aspect terms (e.g., "The screen is clear but small"), nor are there any sentences that do not express opinions about their aspect terms (e.g., "It has a 4.8-inch screen"). Hence, the dataset is not entirely representative of product reviews. By contrast, our datasets, discussed below, contain reviews from three domains, including sentences that express conflicting or no opinions about aspect terms, they concern many more target entities (not just five), and we have also measured inter-annotator agreement.

The dataset of Ganu et al. (2009), on which one of our datasets is based, is also popular. In the original dataset, each sentence is tagged with coarse aspects ('food', 'service', 'price', 'ambience', 'anecdotes', or 'miscellaneous'). For example, "The restaurant was expensive, but the menu was great" would be tagged with the coarse aspects 'price' and 'food'. The coarse aspects, however, are not necessarily terms occurring in the sentence, and it is unclear how they were obtained. By contrast, we asked human annotators to mark the explicit aspect *terms* of each sentence, leaving the task of clustering the terms to produce coarser aspects for an aspect aggregation stage.

The 'Concept-Level Sentiment Analysis Challenge' of ESWC 2014 uses the dataset of Blitzer et al. (2007), which contains customer reviews of

[1]Each aspect term occurrence is also annotated with a sentiment score. We do not discuss these scores here, since we focus on ATE. The same comment applies to the dataset of Ganu et al. (2009) and our datasets.

DVDs, books, kitchen appliances, and electronic products, with an overall sentiment score for each review. One of the challenge's tasks requires systems to extract the aspects of each sentence and a sentiment score (positive or negative) per aspect.[2] The aspects are intended to be concepts from ontologies, not simply aspect terms. The ontologies to be used, however, are not fully specified and no training dataset with sentences and gold aspects is currently available.

Overall, the previous datasets are not entirely satisfactory, because they contain reviews from a particular domain only, or reviews for very few target entities, or their sentences are not entirely representative of customer reviews, or they do not contain annotations for aspect terms, or no inter-annotator agreement has been reported. To address these issues, we provide three new ATE datasets, which contain customer reviews of restaurants, hotels, and laptops, respectively.[3]

2.2 Our datasets

The restaurants dataset contains 3,710 English sentences from the reviews of Ganu et al. (2009).[4] We asked human annotators to tag the aspect terms of each sentence. In "The *dessert* was divine", for example, the annotators would tag the aspect term 'dessert'. In a sentence like "The restaurant was expensive, but the *menu* was great", the annotators were instructed to tag only the explicitly mentioned aspect term 'menu'. The sentence also refers to the prices, and a possibility would be to add 'price' as an *implicit aspect term*, but we do not consider implicit aspect terms in this paper.

We used nine annotators for the restaurant reviews. Each sentence was processed by a single annotator, and each annotator processed approximately the same number of sentences. Among the 3,710 restaurant sentences, 1,248 contain exactly one aspect term, 872 more than one, and 1,590 no aspect terms. There are 593 distinct multi-word aspect terms and 452 distinct single-word aspect terms. Removing aspect terms that occur only once leaves 67 distinct multi-word and 195 distinct single-word aspect terms.

The hotels dataset contains 3,600 English sentences from online customer reviews of 30 hotels. We used three annotators. Among the 3,600 hotel sentences, 1,326 contain exactly one aspect term, 652 more than one, and 1,622 none. There are 199 distinct multi-word aspect terms and 262 distinct single-word aspect terms, of which 24 and 120, respectively, were tagged more than once.

The laptops dataset contains 3,085 English sentences of 394 online customer reviews. A single annotator (one of the authors) was used. Among the 3,085 laptop sentences, 909 contain exactly one aspect term, 416 more than one, and 1,760 none. There are 350 distinct multi-word and 289 distinct single-word aspect terms, of which 67 and 137, respectively, were tagged more than once.

To measure inter-annotator agreement, we used a sample of 75 restaurant, 75 laptop, and 100 hotel sentences. Each sentence was processed by two (for restaurants and laptops) or three (for hotels) annotators, other than the annotators used previously. For each sentence s_i, the inter-annotator agreement was measured as the Dice coefficient $D_i = 2 \cdot \frac{|A_i \cap B_i|}{|A_i| + |B_i|}$, where A_i, B_i are the sets of aspect term occurrences tagged by the two annotators, respectively, and $|S|$ denotes the cardinality of a set S; for hotels, we use the mean pairwise D_i of the three annotators.[5] The overall inter-annotator agreement D was taken to be the average D_i of the sentences of each sample. We, thus, obtained $D = 0.72, 0.70, 0.69$, for restaurants, hotels, and laptops, respectively, which indicate reasonably high inter-annotator agreement.

2.3 Single and multi-word aspect terms

ABSA systems use ATE methods ultimately to obtain the m most prominent (frequently discussed) distinct aspect terms of the target entity, for different values of m.[6] In a system like the one of Fig. 1, for example, if we ignore aspect aggregation, each row will report the average sentiment score of a single frequent distinct aspect term, and m will be the number of rows, which may depend on the display size or user preferences.

Figure 2 shows the percentage of distinct multi-word aspect terms among the m most frequent distinct aspect terms, for different values of m, in

[2] See `http://2014.eswc-conferences.org/`.

[3] Our datasets are available upon request. The datasets of the ABSA task of SemEval 2014 (`http://alt.qcri.org/semeval2014/task4/`) are based on our datasets.

[4] The original dataset of Ganu et al. contains 3,400 sentences, but some of the sentences had not been properly split.

[5] Cohen's Kappa cannot be used here, because the annotators may tag any word sequence of any sentence, which leads to a very large set of categories. A similar problem was reported by Kobayashi et al. (2007).

[6] A more general definition of prominence might also consider the average sentiment score of each distinct aspect term.

our three datasets and the electronics dataset of Hu and Liu (2004). There are many more single-word distinct aspect terms than multi-word distinct aspect terms, especially in the restaurant and hotel reviews. In the electronics and laptops datasets, the percentage of multi-word distinct aspect terms (e.g., 'hard disk') is higher, but most of the distinct aspect terms are still single-word, especially for small values of m. By contrast, many ATE methods (Hu and Liu, 2004; Popescu and Etzioni, 2005; Wei et al., 2010) devote much of their processing to identifying multi-word aspect terms.

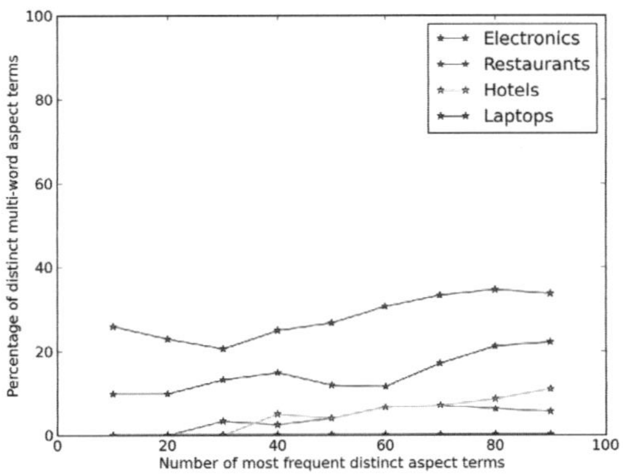

Figure 2: Percentage of (distinct) multi-word aspect terms among the most frequent aspect terms.

3 Evaluation measures

We now discuss previous ATE evaluation measures, also introducing our own.

3.1 Precision, Recall, F-measure

ATE methods are usually evaluated using precision, recall, and F-measure (Hu and Liu, 2004; Popescu and Etzioni, 2005; Kim and Hovy, 2006; Wei et al., 2010; Moghaddam and Ester, 2010; Bagheri et al., 2013), but it is often unclear if these measures are applied to *distinct* aspect terms (no duplicates) or aspect term *occurrences*.

In the former case, each method is expected to return a set A of distinct aspect terms, to be compared to the set G of distinct aspect terms the human annotators identified in the texts. TP (true positives) is $|A \cap G|$, FP (false positives) is $|A \setminus G|$, FN (false negatives) is $|G \setminus A|$, and precision (P), recall (R), $F = \frac{2 \cdot P \cdot R}{P+R}$ are defined as usually:

$$P = \frac{TP}{TP+FP}, \; R = \frac{TP}{TP+FN} \qquad (1)$$

This way, however, precision, recall, and F-measure assign the same importance to all the distinct aspect terms, whereas missing, for example, a more frequent (more frequently discussed) distinct aspect term should probably be penalized more heavily than missing a less frequent one.

When precision, recall, and F-measure are applied to aspect term *occurrences* (Liu et al., 2005), TP is the number of aspect term occurrences tagged (each term occurrence) both by the method being evaluated and the human annotators, FP is the number of aspect term occurrences tagged by the method but not the human annotators, and FN is the number of aspect term occurrences tagged by the human annotators but not the method. The three measures are then defined as above. They now assign more importance to frequently occurring distinct aspect terms, but they can produce misleadingly high scores when only a few, but very frequent distinct aspect terms are handled correctly. Furthermore, the occurrence-based definitions do not take into account that missing several aspect term occurrences or wrongly tagging expressions as aspect term occurrences may not actually matter, as long as the m most frequent distinct aspect terms can be correctly reported.

3.2 Weighted precision, recall, AWP

What the previous definitions of precision and recall miss is that in practice ABSA systems use ATE methods ultimately to obtain the m most frequent distinct aspect terms, for a range of m values. Let A_m and G_m be the *lists* that contain the m most frequent distinct aspect terms, ordered by their predicted and true frequencies, respectively; the predicted and true frequencies are computed by examining how frequently the ATE method or the human annotators, respectively, tagged occurrences of each distinct aspect term. Differences between the predicted and true frequencies do not matter, as long as $A_m = G_m$, for every m. Not including in A_m a term of G_m should be penalized more or less heavily, depending on whether the term's true frequency was high or low, respectively. Furthermore, including in A_m a term not in G_m should be penalized more or less heavily, depending on whether the term was placed towards the beginning or the end of A_m, i.e., depending on the prominence that was assigned to the term.

To address the issues discussed above, we introduce weighted variants of precision and recall.

For each ATE method, we now compute a single *list* $A = \langle a_1, \ldots, a_{|A|} \rangle$ of distinct aspect terms identified by the method, ordered by decreasing predicted frequency. For every m value (number of most frequent distinct aspect terms to show), the method is treated as having returned the sub-list A_m with the first m elements of A. Similarly, we now take $G = \langle g_1, \ldots, g_{|G|} \rangle$ to be the *list* of the distinct aspect terms that the human annotators tagged, ordered by decreasing true frequency.[7] We define weighted precision (WP_m) and weighted recall (WR_m) as in Eq. 2–3. The notation $1\{\kappa\}$ denotes 1 if condition κ holds, and 0 otherwise. By $r(a_i)$ we denote the ranking of the returned term a_i in G, i.e., if $a_i = g_j$, then $r(a_i) = j$; if $a_i \notin G$, then $r(a_i)$ is an arbitrary positive integer.

$$WP_m = \frac{\sum_{i=1}^{m} \frac{1}{i} \cdot 1\{a_i \in G\}}{\sum_{i=1}^{m} \frac{1}{i}} \tag{2}$$

$$WR_m = \frac{\sum_{i=1}^{m} \frac{1}{r(a_i)} \cdot 1\{a_i \in G\}}{\sum_{j=1}^{|G|} \frac{1}{j}} \tag{3}$$

WR_m counts how many terms of G (gold distinct aspect terms) the method returned in A_m, but weighting each term by its inverse ranking $\frac{1}{r(a_i)}$, i.e., assigning more importance to terms the human annotators tagged more frequently. The denominator of Eq. 3 sums the weights of all the terms of G; in unweighted recall applied to distinct aspect terms, where all the terms of G have the same weight, the denominator would be $|G| = TP + FN$ (Eq. 1). WP_m counts how many gold aspect terms the method returned in A_m, but weighting each returned term a_i by its inverse ranking $\frac{1}{i}$ in A_m, to reward methods that return more gold aspect terms towards the beginning of A_m. The denominator of Eq. 2 sums the weights of all the terms of A_m; in unweighted precision applied to distinct aspect terms, the denominator would be $|A_m| = TP + FN$ (Eq. 1).

We plot weighted precision-recall curves by computing WP_m, WR_m pairs for different values of m, as in Fig. 3 below.[8] The higher the curve of a method, the better the method. We also compute the average (interpolated) weighted precision (AWP) of each method over 11 recall levels:

$$AWP = \frac{1}{11} \sum_{r \in \{0, 0.1, \ldots, 1\}} WP_{int}(r)$$

$$WP_{int}(r) = \max_{m \in \{1, \ldots, |A|\},\ WR_m \geq r} WP_m$$

AWP is similar to average (interpolated) precision (AP), which is used to summarize the tradeoff between (unweighted) precision and recall.

3.3 Other related measures

Yu at al. (2011) used $nDCG@m$ (Järvelin and Kekäläinen, 2002; Sakai, 2004; Manning et al., 2008), defined below, to evaluate each list of m distinct aspect terms returned by an ATE method.

$$nDCG@m = \frac{1}{Z} \sum_{i=1}^{m} \frac{2^{t(i)} - 1}{\log_2(1+i)}$$

Z is a normalization factor to ensure that a perfect ranking gets $nDCG@m = 1$, and $t(i)$ is a reward function for a term placed at position i of the returned list. In the work of Yu et al., $t(i) = 1$ if the term at position i is not important (as judged by a human), $t(i) = 2$ if the term is 'ordinary', and $t(i) = 3$ if it is important. The logarithm is used to reduce the reward for distinct aspect terms placed at lower positions of the returned list.

The $nDCG@m$ measure is well known in ranking systems (e.g., search engines) and it is similar to our weighted precision (WP_m). The denominator or Eq. 2 corresponds to the normalization factor Z of $nDCG@m$; the $\frac{1}{i}$ factor of in the numerator of Eq. 2 corresponds to the $\frac{1}{\log_2(1+i)}$ degradation factor of $nDCG@m$; and the $1\{a_i \in G\}$ factor of Eq. 2 is a binary reward function, corresponding to the $2^{t(i)} - 1$ factor of $nDCG@m$.

The main difference from $nDCG@m$ is that WP_m uses a degradation factor $\frac{1}{i}$ that is inversely proportional to the ranking of the returned term a_i in the returned list A_m, whereas $nDCG@m$ uses a logarithmic factor $\frac{1}{\log_2(1+i)}$, which reduces less sharply the reward for distinct aspect terms returned at lower positions in A_m. We believe that the degradation factor of WP_m is more appropriate for ABSA, because most users would in practice wish to view sentiment scores for only a few (e.g., $m = 10$) frequent distinct aspect terms, whereas in search engines users are more likely to examine more of the highly-ranked returned items. It is possible, however, to use a logarithmic degradation factor in WP_m, as in $nDCG@m$.

[7] In our experiments, we exclude from G aspect terms tagged by the annotators only once.

[8] With supervised methods, we perform a 10-fold cross-validation for each m, and we macro-average WP_m, WR_m over the folds. We provide our datasets partitioned in folds.

Another difference is that we use a binary reward factor $1\{a_i \in G\}$ in WP_m, instead of the $2^{t(i)} - 1$ factor of $nDCG@m$ that has three possibly values in the work of Yu at al. (2011). We use a binary reward factor, because preliminary experiments we conducted indicated that multiple relevance levels (e.g., not an aspect term, aspect term but unimportant, important aspect term) confused the annotators and led to lower inter-annotator agreement. The $nDCG@m$ measure can also be used with a binary reward factor; the possible values $t(i)$ would be 0 and 1.

With a binary reward factor, $nDCG@m$ in effect measures the ratio of correct (distinct) aspect terms to the terms returned, assigning more weight to correct aspect terms placed closer the top of the returned list, like WP_m. The $nDCG@m$ measure, however, does not provide any indication of how many of the gold distinct aspect terms have been returned. By contrast, we also measure weighted recall (Eq. 3), which examines how many of the (distinct) gold aspect terms have been returned in A_m, also assigning more weight to the gold aspect terms the human annotators tagged more frequently. We also compute the average weighted precision (AWP), which is a combination of WP_m and WR_m, for a range of m values.

4 Aspect term extraction methods

We implemented and evaluated four ATE methods: (i) a popular baseline (dubbed FREQ) that returns the most frequent distinct nouns and noun phrases, (ii) the well-known method of Hu and Liu (2004), which adds to the baseline pruning mechanisms and steps that detect more aspect terms (dubbed H&L), (iii) an extension of the previous method (dubbed H&L+W2V), with an extra pruning step we devised that uses the recently popular continuous space word vectors (Mikolov et al., 2013c), and (iv) a similar extension of FREQ (dubbed FREQ+W2V). All four methods are *unsupervised*, which is particularly important for ABSA systems intended to be used across domains with minimal changes. They return directly a list A of distinct aspect terms ordered by decreasing predicted frequency, rather than tagging aspect term occurrences, which would require computing the A list from the tagged occurrences before applying our evaluation measures (Section 3.2).

4.1 The FREQ baseline

The FREQ baseline returns the most frequent (distinct) nouns and noun phrases of the reviews in each dataset (restaurants, hotels, laptops), ordered by decreasing sentence frequency (how many sentences contain the noun or noun phrase).[9] This is a reasonably effective and popular baseline (Hu and Liu, 2004; Wei et al., 2010; Liu, 2012).

4.2 The H&L method

The method of Hu and Liu (2004), dubbed H&L, first extracts all the distinct nouns and noun phrases from the reviews of each dataset (lines 3–6 of Algorithm 1) and considers them candidate distinct aspect terms.[10] It then forms longer candidate distinct aspect terms by concatenating pairs and triples of candidate aspect terms occurring in the same sentence, in the order they appear in the sentence (lines 7–11). For example, if 'battery life' and 'screen' occur in the same sentence (in this order), then 'battery life screen' will also become a candidate distinct aspect term.

The resulting candidate distinct aspect terms are ordered by decreasing *p-support* (lines 12–15). The *p-support* of a candidate distinct aspect term t is the number of sentences that contain t, excluding sentences that contain another candidate distinct aspect term t' that subsumes t. For example, if both 'battery life' and 'battery' are candidate distinct aspect terms, a sentence like "The battery life was good" is counted in the *p-support* of 'battery life', but not in the *p-support* of 'battery'.

The method then tries to correct itself by pruning wrong candidate distinct aspect terms and detecting additional candidates. Firstly, it discards multi-word distinct aspect terms that appear in 'non-compact' form in more than one sentences (lines 16–23). A multi-word term t appears in non-compact form in a sentence if there are more than three other words (not words of t) between any two of the words of t in the sentence. For example, the candidate distinct aspect term 'battery life screen' appears in non-compact form in "battery life is way better than screen". Secondly, if the *p-support* of a candidate distinct aspect term t is smaller than 3 and t is subsumed by another can-

[9] We use the default POS tagger of NLTK, and the chunker of NLTK trained on the Treebank corpus; see `http://nltk.org/`. We convert all words to lower-case.

[10] Some details of the work of Hu and Liu (2004) were not entirely clear to us. The discussion here and our implementation reflect our understanding.

didate distinct aspect term t', then t is discarded (lines 21–23).

Subsequently, a set of 'opinion adjectives' is formed; for each sentence and each candidate distinct aspect term t that occurs in the sentence, the closest to t adjective of the sentence (if there is one) is added to the set of opinion adjectives (lines 25-27). The sentences are then re-scanned; if a sentence does not contain any candidate aspect term, but contains an opinion adjective, then the nearest noun to the opinion adjective is added to the candidate distinct aspect terms (lines 28–31). The remaining candidate distinct aspect terms are returned, ordered by decreasing *p-support*.

Algorithm 1 The method of Hu and Liu

```
Require: sentences: a list of sentences
 1: terms = new Set(String)
 2: psupport = new Map(String, int)
 3: for s in sentences do
 4:     nouns = POSTagger(s).getNouns()
 5:     nps = Chunker(s).getNPChunks()
 6:     terms.add(nouns ∪ nps)
 7: for s in sentences do
 8:     for t1, t2 in terms s.t. t1, t2 in s ∧
        s.index(t1)<s.index(t2) do
 9:         terms.add(t1 + " " + t2)
10:     for t1, t2, t3 in s.t. t1, t2,t3 in s ∧
        s.index(t1)<s.index(t2)<s.index(t3) do
11:         terms.add(t1 + " " + t2 + " " + t3)
12: for s in sentences do
13:     for t: t in terms ∧ t in s do
14:         if ¬∃ t': t' in terms ∧ t' in s ∧ t in t' then
15:             psupport[term] += 1
16: nonCompact = new Map(String, int)
17: for t in terms do
18:     for s in sentences do
19:         if maxPairDistance(t.words())>3 then
20:             nonCompact[t] += 1
21: for t in terms do
22:     if nonCompact[t]>1 ∨ (∃ t': t' in terms ∧ t in t' ∧
        psupport[t]<3) then
23:         terms.remove(t)
24: adjs = new Set(String)
25: for s in sentences do
26:     if ∃ t: t in terms ∧ t in s then
27:         adjs.add(POSTagger(s).getNearestAdj(t))
28: for s in sentences do
29:     if ¬∃ t: t in terms ∧ t in s ∧ ∃ a: a in adjs ∧ a in s
        then
30:         t = POSTagger(s).getNearestNoun(adjs)
31:         terms.add(t)
32: return psupport.keysSortedByValue()
```

4.3 The H&L+W2V method

We extended H&L by including an additional pruning step that uses continuous vector space representations of words (Mikolov et al., 2013a; Mikolov et al., 2013b; Mikolov et al., 2013c). The vector representations of the words are produced by using a neural network language model, whose inputs are the vectors of the words occurring in each sentence, treated as latent variables to be learned. We used the English Wikipedia to train the language model and obtain word vectors, with 200 features per vector. Vectors for short phrases, in our case candidate multi-word aspect terms, are produced in a similar manner.[11]

Centroid	Closest Wikipedia words
Com. lang.	only, however, so, way, because
Restaurants	meal, meals, breakfast, wingstreet, snacks
Hotels	restaurant, guests, residence, bed, hotels
Laptops	gameport, hardware, hd floppy, pcs, apple macintosh

Table 1: Wikipedia words closest to the common language and domain centroids.

Our additional pruning stage is invoked immediately immediately after line 6 of Algorithm 1. It uses the ten most frequent candidate distinct aspect terms that are available up to that point (frequency taken to be the number of sentences that contain each candidate) and computes the centroid of their vectors, dubbed the *domain centroid*. Similarly, it computes the centroid of the 20 most frequent words of the Brown Corpus (news category), excluding stop-words and words shorter than three characters; this is the *common language centroid*. Any candidate distinct aspect term whose vector is closer to the common language centroid than the domain centroid is discarded, the intuition being that the candidate names a very general concept, rather than a domain-specific aspect.[12] We use cosine similarity to compute distances. Vectors obtained from Wikipedia are used in all cases.

To showcase the insight of our pruning step, Table 1 shows the five words from the English Wikipedia whose vectors are closest to the common language centroid and the three domain centroids. The words closest to the common language centroid are common words, whereas words closest to the domain centroids name domain-specific concepts that are more likely to be aspect terms.

[11] We use WORD2VEC, available at `https://code.google.com/p/word2vec/`, with a continuous bag of words model, default parameters, the first billion characters of the English Wikipedia, and the pre-processing of `http://mattmahoney.net/dc/textdata.html`.

[12] WORD2VEC does not produce vectors for phrases longer than two words; thus, our pruning mechanism never discards candidate aspect terms of more than two words.

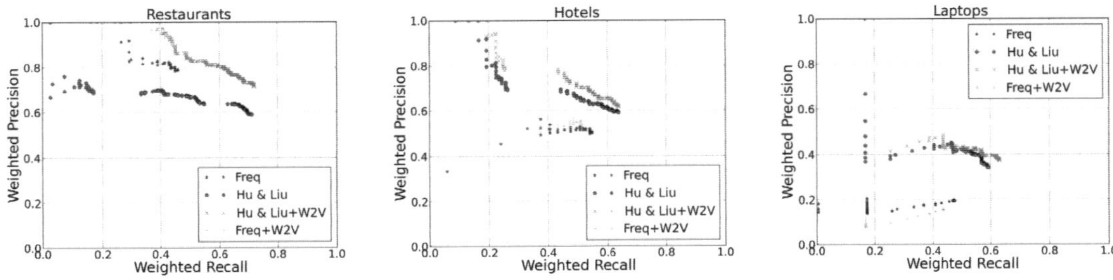

Figure 3: Weighted precision – weighted recall curves for the three datasets.

4.4 The FREQ+W2V method

As with H&L+W2V, we extended FREQ by adding our pruning step that uses the continuous space word (and phrase) vectors. Again, we produced one common language and three domain centroids, as before. Candidate distinct aspect terms whose vector was closer to the common language centroid than the domain centroid were discarded.

5 Experimental results

Table 2 shows the *AWP* scores of the methods. All four methods perform better on the restaurants dataset. At the other extreme, the laptops dataset seems to be the most difficult one; this is due to the fact that it contains many frequent nouns and noun phrases that are not aspect terms; it also contains more multi-word aspect terms (Fig. 2).

H&L performs much better than FREQ in all three domains, and our additional pruning (W2V) improves H&L in all three domains. By contrast FREQ benefits from W2V only in the restaurant reviews (but to a smaller degree than H&L), it benefits only marginally in the hotel reviews, and in the laptop reviews FREQ+W2V performs worse than FREQ. A possible explanation is that the list of candidate (distinct) aspect terms that FREQ produces already misses many aspect terms in the hotel and laptop datasets; hence, W2V, which can only prune aspect terms, cannot improve the results much, and in the case of laptops W2V has a negative effect, because it prunes several correct candidate aspect terms. All differences between *AWP* scores on the same dataset are statistically significant; we use stratified approximate randomization, which indicates $p \leq 0.01$ in all cases.[13]

Figure 3 shows the weighted precision and weighted recall curves of the four methods. In the restaurants dataset, our pruning improves the weighted precision of both H&L and FREQ; by contrast it does not improve weighted recall, since it can only prune candidate aspect terms. The maximum weighted precision of FREQ+W2V is almost as good as that of H&L+W2V, but H&L+W2V (and H&L) reach much higher weighted recall scores. In the hotel reviews, W2V again improves the weighted precision of both H&L and FREQ, but to a smaller extent; again W2V does not improve weighted recall; also, H&L and H&L+W2V again reach higher weighted recall scores. In the laptop reviews, W2V marginally improves the weighted precision of H&L, but it lowers the weighted precision of FREQ; again H&L and H&L+W2V reach higher weighted recall scores. Overall, Fig. 3 confirms that H&L+W2V is the best method.

Method	Restaurants	Hotels	Laptops
FREQ	43.40	30.11	9.09
FREQ+W2V	45.17	30.54	7.18
H&L	52.23	49.73	34.34
H&L+W2V	66.80	53.37	38.93

Table 2: Average weighted precision results (%).

6 Conclusions

We constructed and made publicly available three new ATE datasets from three domains. We also introduced weighted variants of precision, recall, and average precision, arguing that they are more appropriate for ATE. Finally, we discussed how a popular unsupervised ATE method can be improved by adding a new pruning mechanism that uses continuous space vector representations of words and phrases. Using our datasets and evaluation measures, we showed that the improved method performs clearly better than the original one, also outperforming a simpler frequency-based baseline with or without our pruning.

[13] See `http://masanjin.net/sigtest.pdf`.

References

A. Bagheri, M. Saraee, and F. Jong. 2013. An unsupervised aspect detection model for sentiment analysis of reviews. In *Proceedings of NLDB*, volume 7934, pages 140–151.

J. Blitzer, M. Dredze, and F. Pereira. 2007. Biographies, Bollywood, boom-boxes and blenders: Domain adaptation for sentiment classification. In *Proceedings of ACL*, pages 440–447, Prague, Czech Republic.

X. Ding, B. Liu, and P. S. Yu. 2008. A holistic lexicon-based approach to opinion mining. In *Proceedings of WSDM*, pages 231–240, Palo Alto, CA, USA.

G. Ganu, N. Elhadad, and A. Marian. 2009. Beyond the stars: Improving rating predictions using review text content. In *Proceedings of WebDB*, Providence, RI, USA.

M. Hu and B. Liu. 2004. Mining and summarizing customer reviews. In *Proceedings of KDD*, pages 168–177, Seattle, WA, USA.

Kalervo Järvelin and Jaana Kekäläinen. 2002. Cumulated gain-based evaluation of IR techniques. *ACM Transactions on Information Systems*, 20(4):422–446.

S.-M. Kim and E. Hovy. 2006. Extracting opinions, opinion holders, and topics expressed in online news media text. In *Proceedings of SST*, pages 1–8, Sydney, Australia.

N. Kobayashi, K. Inui, and Y. Matsumoto. 2007. Extracting aspect-evaluation and aspect-of relations in opinion mining. In *Proceedings of EMNLP-CoNLL*, pages 1065–1074, Prague, Czech Republic.

B. Liu, M. Hu, and J. Cheng. 2005. Opinion observer: analyzing and comparing opinions on the web. In *Proceedings of WWW*, pages 342–351, Chiba, Japan.

B. Liu. 2012. *Sentiment Analysis and Opinion Mining*. Synthesis Lectures on Human Language Technologies. Morgan & Claypool.

C. Long, J. Zhang, and X. Zhut. 2010. A review selection approach for accurate feature rating estimation. In *Proceedings of COLING*, pages 766–774, Beijing, China.

C. D. Manning, P. Raghavan, and H. Schütze. 2008. *Introduction to Information Retrieval*. Cambridge University Press.

T. Mikolov, K. Chen, G. Corrado, and J. Dean. 2013a. Efficient estimation of word representations in vector space. In *Proceedings of Workshop at ICLR*.

T. Mikolov, I. Sutskever, K. Chen, G. Corrado, and J. Dean. 2013b. Distributed representations of words and phrases and their compositionality. In *Proceedings of NIPS*.

T. Mikolov, W.-T. Yih, and G. Zweig. 2013c. Linguistic regularities in continuous space word representations. In *Proceedings of NAACL HLT*.

S. Moghaddam and M. Ester. 2010. Opinion digger: an unsupervised opinion miner from unstructured product reviews. In *Proceedings of CIKM*, pages 1825–1828, Toronto, ON, Canada.

B. Pang and L. Lee. 2005. Seeing stars: exploiting class relationships for sentiment categorization with respect to rating scales. In *Proceedings of ACL*, pages 115–124, Ann Arbor, MI, USA.

Ana-Maria Popescu and Oren Etzioni. 2005. Extracting product features and opinions from reviews. In *Proceedings of HLT-EMNLP*, pages 339–346, Vancouver, Canada.

T. Sakai. 2004. Ranking the NTCIR systems based on multigrade relevance. In *Proceedings of AIRS*, pages 251–262, Beijing, China.

B. Snyder and R. Barzilay. 2007. Multiple aspect ranking using the good grief algorithm. In *Proceedings of NAACL*, pages 300–307, Rochester, NY, USA.

M. Tsytsarau and T. Palpanas. 2012. Survey on mining subjective data on the web. *Data Mining and Knowledge Discovery*, 24(3):478–514.

C.-P. Wei, Y.-M. Chen, C.-S. Yang, and C. C Yang. 2010. Understanding what concerns consumers: a semantic approach to product feature extraction from consumer reviews. *Information Systems and E-Business Management*, 8(2):149–167.

J. Yu, Z. Zha, M. Wang, and T. Chua. 2011. Aspect ranking: identifying important product aspects from online consumer reviews. In *Proceedings of NAACL*, pages 1496–1505, Portland, OR, USA.

Z. Zhai, B. Liu, H. Xu, and P. Jia. 2010. Grouping product features using semi-supervised learning with soft-constraints. In *Proceedings of COLING*, pages 1272–1280, Beijing, China.

Z. Zhai, B. Liu, H. Xu, and P. Jia. 2011. Clustering product features for opinion mining. In *Proceedings of WSDM*, pages 347–354, Hong Kong, China.

Vowel and Diacritic Restoration for Social Media Texts

Kübra Adalı
Dep. of Computer Eng.
Istanbul Technical University
Istanbul, Turkey
kubraadali@itu.edu.tr

Gülşen Eryiğit
Dep. of Computer Eng.
Istanbul Technical University
Istanbul, Turkey
gulsen.cebiroglu@itu.edu.tr

Abstract

In this paper, we focus on two important problems of social media text normalization, namely: vowel and diacritic restoration. For these two problems, we propose a hybrid model consisting both a discriminative sequence classifier and a language validator in order to select one of the morphologically valid outputs of the first stage. The proposed model is language independent and has no need for manual annotation of the training data. We measured the performance both on synthetic data specifically produced for these two problems and on real social media data. Our model (with 97.06% on synthetic data) improves the state of the art results for diacritization of Turkish by 3.65 percentage points on ambiguous cases and for the vowel restoration by 45.77 percentage points over a rule based baseline with 62.66% accuracy. The results on real data are 95.43% and 69.56% accordingly.

1 Introduction

In recent years, with the high usage of computers and social networks like Facebook and Twitter, the analysis of the social media language has become a very popular and crucial form of business intelligence. But unfortunately, this language is very different from the well edited written texts and much more similar to the spoken language, so that, the available NLP tools do not perform well on this new platform.

As we all know, Twitter announced (at April 1st, 2013)[1] that it is shifting to a two-tiered service where the basic free service 'Twttr" will only allow to use consonants in the tweets. Although, this is a very funny joke, people nowadays are already very used to use this style of writing without vowels in order to fit their messages into 140 characters Twitter or 160 characters SMS messages. As a result, the vowelization problem (Twttr $\Rightarrow$ Twitter) is no more limited with some specific language families (e.g.semitic languages) (Gal, 2002; Zitouni et al., 2006) but it became a problem of social media text normalization in general.

Diacritics are some marks (e.g. accents, dots, curves) added to the characters and have a wide usage in many languages. The absence of these marks in Web2.0 language is very common and posses a big problem in the automatic processing of this data by NLP tools. Although, in the literature, the term "diacritization" is used both for vowel and diacritic restoration for semitic languages, in this paper, we use this term only for the task of converting an ASCII text to its proper form (with accents and special characters). A Turkish example is the word "dondu" (*it is frozen*) which may be the ascii form of both "dondu"(*it is frozen*) or "döndü" (*it returned*) where the ambiguity should be resolved according to the context. In some studies, this task is also referred as "unicodification"(Scannell, 2011) or "deasciification"(Tür, 2000).

In this paper, we focus on these two important problems of social text normalization, namely: diacritization and vowelization. These two problems compose almost the quarter (26.5%) of the normalization errors within a 25K Turkish Tweeter Data Set. We propose a two stage hybrid model: firstly a discriminative model as a sequence classification task by using CRFs (Conditional Random Fields) and secondly a language validator over the first stage's results. Although in this paper, we presented our results on Turkish (which is a highly agglutinative language with very long words full of un-ascii characters), the proposed model is totally language independent and has no need for manual

[1] https://blog.twitter.com/2013/annncng-twttr

annotation of the training data. For morphologically simpler languages, it would be enough to use a lexicon lookup for the language validation stage (whereas we used a morphological analyzer for the case of Turkish). With our proposed model, we obtained the highest results in the literature for Turkish diacritization and vowelization.

The remaining of the paper is structured as follows: Section 2 discusses the related work, Section 3 tries to show the complexity of diacritization and the vowelization tasks by giving examples from an agglutinative language; Turkish. Section 4 introduces our proposed model and Section 5 presents our experiments and results. The conclusion is given in Section 6.

2 Related Work

The vowelization problem is mostly studied for semitic languages and many different methods are applied to this problem. The problem is generally referred as diacritization for these languages, since diacritics are placed on consonants for the purpose of vowel restoration. For example, the short vowels in Arabic are only pronounced by the use of diacritics put on other consonants. Some of these studies are as follows: Gal (2002) reports the results on Hebrew by using HMMs and Zitouni et al. (2006) on Arabic by using maximum entropy based models. Al-Shareef and Hain (Al-Shareef and Hain, 2012) deals with the vowelization of colloquial Arabic for automatic speech recognition task by using CRFs on speaker and contextual information. Haertel et al. (2010) uses conditional markov models for the vowel restoration problem of Syriac. Nelken and Shieber (2005) uses a finite state transducer approach for Arabic as well. To the best of our knowledge, the vowelization work on Turkish is the first study on a language which do not possess the vowelization problem by its nature. We believe that on that sense, our hybrid model will be a good reference for future studies in social media text normalization where the problem is disregarded in recent studies.

The diacritization task on the other hand is not addressed as frequently as the vowelization problem[2]. Some studies are as follows: Scannell (2011) uses a Naive Bayes classifier for both word-level and character-level modeling. Each ambiguous character in the input is regarded as an independent classification problem. They are using lexicon lookup which is not feasible for every possible word surface form in agglutinative or highly inflected languages. They refer to a language model in ambiguous cases. They tested their system for 115 languages as well as for Turkish (92.8% on a much easier data set than ours (refer to Section 5.1) . Simard and Deslauriers (2001) tries to recover the missing accents in French. They are using a generative statistical model for this purpose. De Pauw et al. (2007) also test their MBL (memory based learning) model on different languages. Although they do not test for Turkish, the most attractive part of theirs results is that the performances for highly inflectional languages differ sharply from the others towards the negative side. Nguyen and Ock (2010) deals with the diacritization of Vietnamese by using Adaboost and C4.5.

The work done so far for the diacritization of Turkish are from Tür (2000) (character-based HMM model), Zemberek (2007), Yüret and de la Maza (Yüret and de la Maza, 2006) (GPA: a kind of decision list algorithms). We give the comparison of the two later systems on our data set and propose a discriminative equivalent of the HMM approach used in Tür (2000) (see Section 5 for further discussions). For the vowelization, the only study that we could find is from Tür (2000) which uses again the same character-level HMM model into this problem (with an equivalent discriminative model given at Table 8 $\pm$3ch model).

3 The complexity

This section tries to draw light upon the complexity of diacritization and the vowelization tasks by giving examples from an agglutinative language; Turkish.

3.1 Turkish

Turkish is an agglutinative language which means that words have theoretically an infinite number of possible surface forms due to the iterative concatenation of inflectional and derivational suffixes. As for other similar languages, this property of the language makes impractical for Turkish words to be validated by using a lexicon. And also, the increasing length[3] of the words creates a big search space especially for the vowelization task.

[2]Here, we exclude all the works done for semitic languages. The reason is explained on the former paragraph.

[3]The average word length is calculated as 6.1 for Turkish nouns and 7.6 for verbs in a 5 million word corpus(Akın and Akın, 2007).

Turkish alphabet has 7 non-ascii characters that don't exist in the Latin alphabet (ç, ğ, ı, İ, ö, ş, ü) and the ascii counterparts of these letters (c, g, i, I, o, s, u) are also valid letters in the alphabet which causes an important disambiguation problem at both word and sentence level. The alphabet contains 8 vowels (a(A), e(E), ı(I), i(İ), o(O), ö(Ö), u(U), ü(Ü)) in total.

3.2 Diacritization

The following real example sentence taken from social media "Ruyamda evde oldugunu gordum.", written by using only the ascii alphabet, has two possible valid diacritized versions:

1. "Rüyamda evde olduğunu gördüm."
(*I had a dream that you were at home.*)

2. "Rüyamda evde öldüğünü gördüm."
(*I had a dream that you died at home.*)

As can be observed from this sentence some of the asciified words (e.g. "oldugunu") has more than one possible valid counterparts which causes the meaning change of the whole sentence.

The problem is the decision of the appropriate forms for the critical letters (C, G, I, O, S, U)[4]. Although the problem seems like a multi-class classification problem, it is in essence a binary-classification task for each critical letter and can be viewed as a binary sequence classification task for the whole word so that the original word will be chosen from (2^n) possibilities where n is the number of occurrence of critical letters (C, G, I, O, S, U) in the ascii version. For example the word "OldUGUnU" has (2^5=32) possible transformations whereas only 2 of them ("olduğunu" and "öldüğünü") are valid Turkish words. Figure 1 gives a second example and shows all the possible (2^2=4) diacritized versions of the word "aCI" where again only two of them are valid words (emphasized with a bold background colour): "açı"(*angle*) and "acı"(*pain*).

3.3 Vowelization

Vowelization on the other hand causes much more complexity when compared to diacritization. Each position[5] between consequent consonants, at the beginning or ending of the word may take one vowel or not resulting a selection from 9 class labels (the 8 vowel letters + the null character). For example, the vowelization of the word "slm"("*hi*" written without vowels, with n=4 positions _s_l_m_) will produce 9^4 = 6561 possibilities where 39 of them are valid Turkish words (e.g. "salam"(*salami*), "sulama"(*watering*), "salım"(*my raft*), "selam"(*hi*), "sılam"(*my furlough*) etc...).

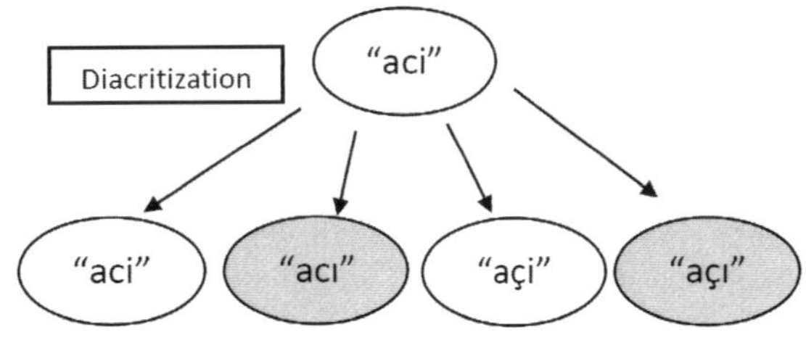

Figure 1: Possible Diacritized Versions of "aCI"

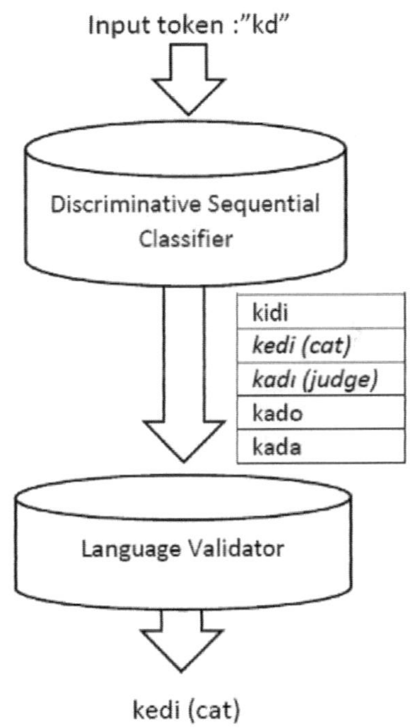

Figure 2: Proposed Model

4 Proposed Model

Most of the previous work in the literature (Section 2) uses either some (generative of discriminative) machine learning models or some nlp tools (e.g. morphological analyzers, pos taggers, linguistic rules) in order to solve the vowelization

[4]From this point on, we will show the ascii versions of these letters as capital letters meaning that they may appear in the diacritized version of the word either in their ascii form or in their diacritized form. Ex: the capital C will become either c or ç after the processing.

[5]For the sake of simplicity, we just assumed that only zero or one vowel may appear between two consonants whereas there exist some words with consecutive vowels (such as "saat"(*clock*)) although very rarely

problem. As it is shown in the previous section, for languages with higher number of vowels and word length due to their rich inflectional morphology, the search space gets very high very rapidly. Since the problem is mostly similar to generation, in order to increase the likelihood of the generated output word, most of the approaches include character level probabilities or relationships. In this case, it is unfair to expect from a machine learning system to generate morphologically valid outputs (especially for highly inflectional languages) while trying to maximize the overall character sequence probability.

We propose a two stage model (Figure 2) which has basically two components.

1. a discriminative sequence classifier
2. a language validator

4.1 Discriminative Sequence Classifier

In the first stage, we use CRFs[6] (Lafferty et al., 2001) in order to produce the most probable output words. This stage treats the diacritization and vowelization as character level sequence labeling tasks, but since it is a discriminative model, it is also possible to provide neighboring words as features into the system. During training, each instance within a sequence has basically the following main parts:

1. features related to the current and neighboring tokens (namely surface form or lemma)
2. features related to the current and neighboring characters[8]
3. class label

The test data is also prepared similarly except the gold standard class labels.

Table 1 and Table 2 show instance samples for the sample words ("OldUGUnU" and "_s_l_m_ ") given in Section 3. As can be observed from the tables, we have 7 different class labels in diacritic restoration and 9 different class labels in vowel restoration (one can refer to Section 3 for the details). The sequences represent words in focus and each instance line within a sequence stands for the character position in focus. The sample for diacritization has 5 character features and 2 word features where the current character feature limits the number of the class labels to be assigned to that position by 2. The sample for vowelization has 1 word feature and 6 character features.

Curr. Letter	Neig. Word(+1)	Curr. Word	Neig. Ch(-2)	Neig. Ch(-1)	Neig. Ch(+1)	Neig. Ch(+2)	Class Label
O	GOrdUm	OldUGUnU	_	_	l	d	ö
U	GOrdUm	OldUGUnU	l	d	G	U	ü
G	GOrdUm	OldUGUnU	d	U	U	n	ğ
U	GOrdUm	OldUGUnU	U	G	n	U	ü
U	GOrdUm	OldUGUnU	U	n	_	_	ü

Table 1: Diacritization: Instance Representation for the word "oldugunu"
"OldUGUnU" 5 critical positions

Curr. Word	Neig. Ch(-3)	Neig. Ch(-2)	Neig. Ch(-1)	Neig. Ch(+1)	Neig. Ch(+2)	Neig. Ch(+3)	Class Label
slm	_	_	_	s	l	m	_
slm	_	_	s	l	m	_	e
slm	_	s	l	m	_	_	a
slm	s	l	m	_	_	_	_

Table 2: Vowelization: Instance Representation for the word "slm"
"_s_l_m_" 4 possible vowel positions

CRFs are log-linear models and in order to get advantage of the useful feature combinations, one needs to provide these as new features to the CRFs. In order to adopt a systematic way, we took the features' combinations for character features and word features separately. For character features we took the combinations up to 6-grams for $\pm$3ch and for the neighboring word features up to 4 grams. The number of features affects directly the maximum amount of training data that could be used during the experiments. The total number of feature templates after the addition of feature combinations ranges between 7 for the simplest case and 30 for our model with maximum number of features. Three sample feature templates are given below for the sample sequence of Table 1. The templates are given in [pos,col] format, where pos stands for the relative position of the token in focus and col stands for the feature column number in the input file. U06 is the template for using the sixth[9] feature in Table 1 (Neigh. Ch(+1)). U13 is a bigram feature combination of 2nd and 3th features (the current token and the next token). U11 is a fourgram feature combination of 4th, 5th, 6th and 7th features of our feature set that refers to the group of the previous two characters and the next two characters.

[6]In this work, we used CRF++[7] which is an open source implementation of CRFs.

[8]The feature related to the current character is only available in diacritization model

[9]in CRF++ feature templates the features indexes start from 0.

$$U06 : \%x[0,5]$$

$$U13 : \%x[0,1]/\%x[0,2]$$

$$U11 : \%x[0,3]/\%x[0,4]/\%x[0,5]/\%x[0,6]$$

4.2 Language Validator

The n best sequences of the discriminative classifier is then transferred to the language validator. We use a two-level morphological analyzer (Şahin et al., 2013) for the Turkish case since in this agglutinative language it is impractical to validate a word by making a lexicon lookup. But this second part may be replaced by any language validator (for other languages) which will filter only the valid outputs from the n best results of the discriminative classifier. Figure 2 shows an example case of the process for vowelization. The system takes the consonant sequence "kd" and the 5 best output of the first stage is produced as "kidi, kedi, kadı, kado, kada". The language validator then chooses the most probable valid word "kedi" (*cat*) as its output. One should notice that if none of the n most probable results is a valid word, then the system won't produce any suggestion at all. We show experimental results on the effect of the selection of n in the next section.

5 Experimental Setup And Results

In this section, we first present our datasets and evaluation strategy. We then continue with the diacritization experiments and finally we share the results of our vowelization experiments.

5.1 Datasets and Evaluation Methodology

For both of the diacritization and vowelization tasks, creating the labeled data is a straightforward task since the reverse operations for these (converting from formally written text to their Ascii form or to a form without vowels) can be accomplished automatically for most of the languages (except semitic languages where the vowels do not appear in the formal form). To give an example from Turkish, the word "olduğunu" may be automatically converted to the form "OldUGUnU" for diacritization and "_l_d_g_n_" for vowelization experiments. We used data from three different corpora: METU Corpus (Say et al., 2002) and two web corpora from Yıldız and Tantuğ (2012) and Sak et al. (2011).

In order to judge different approaches fairly, we aimed to create a decently though test set. Since the vowelization task already comprises a very high ambiguity, we focused to the ambiguous diacritization samples. With this purpose, we first took the Turkish dictionary and converted all the lemmas within the dictionary into their Ascii forms. We then created the possible diacritized forms (Figure 1) and created a list of all ambiguous lemmas (1221 lemmas in total) by finding all the lemmas which could be produced as the output of diacritization. For example "açı" and "acı" are put into this list after this operation. Although this ambiguous lemmas list may be extended by also considering interfusing surface forms, for the sake of simplicity we just considered to take the ambiguous lemmas from the dictionary. We then searched our three corpora (and the WEB where not available in these) for the words with an ambiguous lemma and created our test set so that for each ambiguous lemma there is exactly one sentence consisting of it. As a result, we collected a test set of 1157 sentences (17923 tokens) consisting of 1871 ambiguous words[10] in total. The remaining sentences from the corpora are used during training. Since the feature set size directly affects the amount of usable training data, for different experiment sets we used different size of training data each time trying to use the data from the three corpora in equal amounts.

After evaluating with synthetically produced training and test sets, we also tested our best performed models on real data collected from social media (25K tweets with at least one erroneous token) and normalized manually (Eryiğit et al., 2013). This data consists 58836 tokens that have text normalization problems where 3.75% is due to missing vowels and 22.8% is due to misuse of Turkish characters. In order to separate these specific error sets, we first automatically aligned the original and normalized tweets and then applied some filters over the aligned data: e.g. Deascification errors are selected so that the character length of the original word and its normalized form should be the same and the differing letters should only be the versions of the same Turkish characters.

For the evaluation of diacritization, we provide two accuracy scores: Accuracy over the entire words ($Acc_{Overall}$ Equation 1) and accuracy over the ambiguous words alone (Acc_{Amb} Equation 2

[10] One should note that each sentence in the test set contains at least one or more ambiguous surface forms. The test data will be available to the researches via http://...

over 1871 ambiguous words in the test set). Since the vowelization problem is almost entirely ambiguous, the two scores are almost the same for the entire tests ($\# \ of \ words \approx \# \ of \ amb. \ words$). That is why, for the vowelization task we provide only $Acc_{Overall}$.

$$Acc_{Overall} = \frac{\# \ of \ corr. \ diacritized \ words}{\# \ of \ words} \quad (1)$$

$$Acc_{Amb} = \frac{\# \ of \ corr. \ diacritized \ amb. \ words}{\# \ of \ amb. \ words} \quad (2)$$

In the work of Tür (2000), the accuracy score is provided as the correctly determined characters which we do not find useful for the given tasks: $Acc_{Amb} = \frac{\# \ of \ corr. \ diacritized \ amb. \ chars}{\# \ of \ amb. \ chars}$. This score gives credit to the systems although the produced output word is not a valid Turkish word. For example, if a vowelization system produces an invalid output as "oldgn" for the input "_l_d_g_n_", it will have a 1/5 (one correct character over 5 possible positions) score whereas in our evaluation this output will be totally penalized.

5.2 Diacritization Experiments

For diacritization, we designed four sets of experiments. The first set of experiments (Table 3) presents the results of our baseline systems. We provide four baseline systems. The first one is a rule based diacritics restorer which creates all the possible diacritics for a given input and outputs the first morphologically valid one. As the proposed model does, the rule based system also validates its outputs by using the morphological analyzer introduced in Section 4.2. One can see from the table that the accuracy on the ambiguous words of this system is nearly 70%. Our second baseline uses a unigram language model in order to select the most probable valid output of the morphological analyzer. Our third baseline is a baseline for our discriminative classifier (with only ±2 neighboring characters) without the language validator component. In this model, the top most output of the CRF is accepted as the correct output word. One can observe that this baseline although it performs better than the rule based system, it is worse than the second baseline with a language model component. Our last baseline is the baseline for the proposed system in this paper with a discriminative classifier (using only ±2 neighboring characters) and a language validator which chooses the first valid output within the top 5 results of the classifier. It outperforms all the previous baselines.

System	Acc Overall	Acc Amb
Rule based	90.38	69.17
Rule based + Unigram LM	91.94	83.54
CRF $\pm 2ch$	87.93	77.24
CRF ±2ch + Lang.Valid.	**94.88**	**88.51**

Table 3: Diacritization Baseline Results

The second set of experiments given in Table 4 is for the feature selection of the proposed model. We test with the neighboring characters up to ±3 and together with the surface form of the current token $sform_{curr}$ and/or the first n characters of the current token $firstnch_{curr}$ as lemma feature. For both of the first two sets of experiments (Table 3 and Table 4) we used a training data of size 4591K (the max. possible size for the most complex feature set in these experiments; (last line of Table 4). It can be observed from Table 4 that although ±3ch (2nd line) performs better than ±2ch (1st line), when we use these together with $sform_{curr}$ we obtain better results with ±2ch (3rd line). Since ±3ch (7 characters in total) will be very close to the whole number of characters within the surface form, the new feature's help is more modest in ±3ch model. In these experiments we try to optimize on the overall accuracies. Our highest score in this table is with the $\pm 2ch + sform_{curr} + first5ch_{curr}$ (last line) but since the difference between this and $\pm 2ch + sform_{curr}$ is not statistically significant (with McNemar's test $p<0.01$) and the size of the maximum possible training data could still be improved for the latter model, we decided to continue with $\pm 2ch + sform_{curr}$.

In the third set of diacritization experiments (Table 5) we investigated the effect of using the neighboring tokens as features. In this experiment set, the training data size is decreased to a much lower size, only 971K in order to be able to train with ±2 neighboring tokens. Each line of the table is the addition of the surface forms for the precised positions to the model of the first line $\pm 2ch + sform_{curr}$. We tested with all the combinations in the ±2 window size. For exam-

Feature Combinations	Acc Overall	Acc Amb
$\pm 2ch$	94.88	88.51
$\pm 3ch$	95.76	91.05
$\pm$2ch + sform$_{\mathbf{curr}}$	**96.26**	**91.60**
$\pm 3ch + sform_{curr}$	96.20	91.71
$\pm 2ch + first3ch_{curr}$	95.29	90.17
$\pm 2ch + first4ch_{curr}$	95.60	89.06
$\pm 2ch + first5ch_{curr}$	95.95	90.72
$\pm 2ch + sform_{curr} + first3ch_{curr}$	96.23	91.82
$\pm 2ch + sform_{curr} + first4ch_{curr}$	96.26	91.82
$\pm 2ch + sform_{curr} + first5ch_{curr}$	96.28	91.60

Table 4: Diacritization Feature Selection I

Features	Acc Overall	Acc Amb
$\pm 2ch + sform_{curr}$	95.29	90.61
+sform$_{\mathbf{0010}}$	**95.49**	**90.72**
$+sform_{0011}$	95.39	90.39
$+sform_{0100}$	93.77	83.32
$+sform_{0110}$	95.39	90.28
$+sform_{0111}$	95.26	89.95
$+sform_{1100}$	95.24	89.83
$+sform_{1110}$	95.21	89.50
$+sform_{1111}$	95.11	89.17

Table 5: Diacritization Feature Selection II

ple $sform_{0010}$ means that the surface form of the token at position +1 is added to the features. This feature set outperformed all the other ones.

System	Acc Overall	Acc Amb
Yüret (2006)	95.93	91.05
Zemberek (2007)	87.71	82.55
$\pm 2ch + sform_{curr}$	96.15	92.04
$\pm$2ch + sform$_{\mathbf{curr}}$ + sform$_{\mathbf{0010}}$	**97.06**	**94.70**

Table 6: Diacritization Results Comparison with Previous Work

Finally, in Table 6, we give the comparison results of our proposed model with the available Turkish deasciifiers (the tools' original name given by the authors) (Yüret and de la Maza, 2006; Akın and Akın, 2007). We both tested by $\pm 2ch + sform_{curr}$ and $\pm 2ch + sform_{curr} + sform_{0010}$. Both of the models are tested with maximum possible size of training data: 10379K and 5764K successively. Our proposed model for diacritization outperformed all of the other methods with a success rate of 97.06%. It outperformed the state of the art by 1.13 percentage points in overall accuracy and by 3.65 percentage points in ambiguous cases (both results statistically significant).

5.3 Vowelization Experiments

For the vowelization, we designed similar set of experiments. In Table 7, we provide the results for a rulebased baseline and our proposed model with $\pm 2ch$. It is certainly a very time consuming process to produce all the possible forms for the vowelization task (see Section 3.3). Thus, for the rule based baseline we stopped the generation process once we find a valid output. The baseline of the proposed model provides a 28.44 percentage points improvements over the rule based system. We did not try to compare our results with the work of Tür (2000) (an HMM model on character level) firstly because the developed model was not available for testing, secondly because the provided evaluation (see Section 5.1) was useless for our purposes and finally because our ± 3 character model provided in the second line of Table 8 is a discriminative counterpart of his 6-gram generative model.

System	Acc Overall
Rule based	16.89
CRF $\pm$2ch+Lang.Valid.	**45.33**

Table 7: Vowelization Baseline Results

Table 8 gives the feature selection tests' results similarly to the previous section. This time we obtained the highest score with $\pm 3ch + sform_{curr}$ 59.17%. In this set of experiments, we used 4445K of training data.

In order to investigate the impact of neighboring tokens, in the experiments given in Table 9, we had to continue with $\pm 2ch + sform_{curr}$ with

Feature Combinations	Acc Overall
$\pm 2ch$	45.33
$\pm 3ch$	57.20
$\pm 2ch + sform_{curr}$	57.22
$\pm$3ch + sform$_{\mathbf{curr}}$	**59.17**
$\pm 2ch + first3ch_{curr}$	40.44
$\pm 2ch + first4ch_{curr}$	40.48
$\pm 2ch + first5ch_{curr}$	44.22
$\pm 2ch + sform_{curr} + first3ch_{curr}$	45.89
$\pm 2ch + sform_{curr} + first4ch_{curr}$	45.89
$\pm 2ch + sform_{curr} + first5ch_{curr}$	49.58

Table 8: Vowelization Feature Selection I

Features	Acc Overall
$\pm$**2ch** + **sform**$_{\mathbf{curr}}$	**54.07**
$+sform_{0010}$	50.89
$+sform_{0011}$	49.60
$+sform_{0100}$	31.84
$+sform_{0110}$	49.41
$+sform_{0111}$	47.78
$+sform_{1100}$	48.98
$+sform_{1110}$	47.88
$+sform_{1111}$	47.21

Table 9: Vowelization Feature Selection II

971K of training data.[11] We could not obtain any improvement with the neighboring tokens. We relate these results to the fact that the neighboring tokens are also in vowel-less form in the training data so that this information do not help the disambiguation of the current token. Since we could not add the word based features to this task by this model, for future work we are planning to apply a word based language model over the proposed model's possible output sequences.

In the final experiment set given in Table 10, we trained our best performing model $\pm 3ch + sform_{curr}$ with the maximum possible training data (6653K). We also tested with different N values of CRF output. Although there is a slight increase on the overall accuracy by passing from N=5 to N=10, the increase is much higher when we evaluate with Acc_{topN}. Equation 3 gives the calculation of this score which basically calculates the highest score that could be obtained after perfect reranking of the top N results. In this score the system is credited if the correct vowelized answer is within the top N results of the system. We see from the table that there is still a margin for the improvement in top 10 results (up to 85.09% for the best model). This strengthens our believe for the need of a word based language model over the proposed model outputs. Our vowelization model in its current state achieves an accuracy score of 62.66% with a 45.77 percentage points improvements over the rule based baseline.

[11] If we select the larger model, it is going to be impossible to feed enough training data to the system. Since in this set of experiments (Table 9) we only investigate the impact of neighboring tokens, we had/preferred to select the smaller character model.

$$Acc_{topN} = \frac{\sum 1\ if\ result\ exists\ within\ top\ N}{\#\ of\ words} \quad (3)$$

System	Acc Overall	Acc top N
$\pm 3ch + sform_{curr}$ With Top 5 Poss. from CRF	62.05	80.21
$\pm 3ch + sform_{curr}$ With Top 7 Poss. from CRF	62.36	82.53
$\pm 3ch + sform_{curr}$ With Top 10 Poss. from CRF	**62.66**	**85.09**

Table 10: Vowelization Top N Results

Finally we test our best models on vowelization and diacritization errors from our Tweeter data set and obtained 95.43% for diacritization and 69.56% for vowelization.

6 Conclusion And Future Work

In this paper, we proposed a hybrid model for the diacritization and vowelization tasks which is an emerging problem of social media text normalization. Although the tasks are previously investigated for different purposes especially for semitic languages, to the best of our knowledge, this is the first time that they are evaluated together for the social media data on a language which do not possess these problems in its formal form but only in social media platform. We obtained the highest scores for the diacritization (97.06%) and vowelization (62.66%) of Turkish.

We have two future plans for the vowelization part of the proposed model. The first one, as detailed in previous section, is the application of a word based language model over the valid CRF outputs. The second one is the extension for partial vowelization. Although in this work, we designed the vowelization task as the overall generation of the entire vowels within a vowel-less word, we observe from the social web data that people also tend to write with partially missing vowels. As an example, they are writing "sevyrm" instead of the word "seviyorum" (*I love*). In this case, the position between the consonants 's' and 'v' is constrained to the letter 'e' and it is meaningless to generate the other possibilities for the remaining 7 vowels. For this task, we are planning to focus on constrained Viterbi algorithms during the decoding stage.

The tool's web api and the produced data sets will be available to the researchers from the following address http://tools.nlp.itu.edu.tr/(Eryiğit, 2014)

Acknowledgment

This work is part of a research project supported by TUBITAK 1001(Grant number: 112E276) as an ICT cost action (IC1207) project.

References

Ahmet Afsin Akın and Mehmet Dündar Akın. 2007. Zemberek, an open source nlp framework for turkic languages. *Structure*.

Sarah Al-Shareef and Thomas Hain. 2012. Crf-based diacritisation of colloquial Arabic for automatic speech recognition. In *INTERSPEECH*. ISCA.

Guy De Pauw, Peter W. Wagacha, and Gilles-Maurice de Schryver. 2007. Automatic diacritic restoration for resource-scarce languages. In *Proceedings of the 10th international conference on Text, speech and dialogue*, TSD'07, pages 170–179, Berlin, Heidelberg. Springer-Verlag.

Gülşen Eryiğit, Fatih Samet Çetin, Meltem Yanık, Tanel Temel, and İyas Çiçekli. 2013. Turksent: A sentiment annotation tool for social media. In *Proceedings of the 7th Linguistic Annotation Workshop and Interoperability with Discourse*, pages 131–134, Sofia, Bulgaria, August. Association for Computational Linguistics.

Gülşen Eryiğit. 2014. ITU Turkish NLP web service. In *Proceedings of the Demonstrations at the 14th Conference of the European Chapter of the Association for Computational Linguistics (EACL)*, Gothenburg, Sweden, April. Association for Computational Linguistics.

Ya'akov Gal. 2002. An hmm approach to vowel restoration in Arabic and Hebrew. In *Proceedings of the ACL-02 workshop on Computational approaches to semitic languages*, SEMITIC '02, pages 1–7, Stroudsburg, PA, USA. Association for Computational Linguistics.

Robbie A. Haertel, Peter McClanahan, and Eric K. Ringger. 2010. Automatic diacritization for low-resource languages using a hybrid word and consonant cmm. In *Human Language Technologies: The 2010 Annual Conference of the North American Chapter of the Association for Computational Linguistics*, HLT '10, pages 519–527, Stroudsburg, PA, USA. Association for Computational Linguistics.

John D. Lafferty, Andrew McCallum, and Fernando C. N. Pereira. 2001. Conditional random fields: Probabilistic models for segmenting and labeling sequence data. In *ICML*, pages 282–289.

Rani Nelken and Stuart M. Shieber. 2005. Arabic diacritization using weighted finite-state transducers. In *Proceedings of the ACL Workshop on Computational Approaches to Semitic Languages*, Semitic '05, pages 79–86, Stroudsburg, PA, USA. Association for Computational Linguistics.

Kiem-Hieu Nguyen and Cheol-Young Ock. 2010. Diacritics restoration in Vietnamese: letter based vs. syllable based model. In *Proceedings of the 11th Pacific Rim international conference on Trends in artificial intelligence*, PRICAI'10, pages 631–636, Berlin, Heidelberg. Springer-Verlag.

Muhammet Şahin, Umut Sulubacak, and Gülşen Eryiğit. 2013. Redefinition of Turkish morphology using flag diacritics. In *Proceedings of The Tenth Symposium on Natural Language Processing (SNLP-2013)*, Phuket, Thailand, October.

Haşim Sak, Tunga Güngör, and Murat Saraçlar. 2011. Resources for Turkish morphological processing. *Lang. Resour. Eval.*, 45(2):249–261, May.

Bilge Say, Deniz Zeyrek, Kemal Oflazer, and Umut Özge. 2002. Development of a corpus and a treebank for present-day written Turkish. In *Proceedings of the Eleventh International Conference of Turkish Linguistics*, Famaguste, Cyprus, August.

Kevin P. Scannell. 2011. Statistical unicodification of African languages. *Lang. Resour. Eval.*, 45(3):375–386, September.

Michel Simard and Alexandre Deslauriers. 2001. Real-time automatic insertion of accents in French text. *Nat. Lang. Eng.*, 7(2):143–165, June.

Gökhan Tür. 2000. *A statistical information extraction system for Turkish*. Ph.D. thesis, Department of Computer Engineering and the Institute of Engineering and Science of Bilkent University, Ankara.

Eray Yıldız and Cüneyd Tantuğ. 2012. Evaluation of sentence alignment methods for English-Turkish parallel texts. In *Proceedings of the First Workshop on Language Resources and Technologies for Turkic Languages (LREC)*, Istanbul, Turkey, 23-25 May.

Deniz Yüret and Michael de la Maza. 2006. The greedy prepend algorithm for decision list induction. In *Proceedings of the 21st international conference on Computer and Information Sciences*, ISCIS'06, pages 37–46, Berlin, Heidelberg. Springer-Verlag.

Imed Zitouni, Jeffrey S. Sorensen, and Ruhi Sarikaya. 2006. Maximum entropy based restoration of Arabic diacritics. In *Proceedings of the 21st International Conference on Computational Linguistics and the 44th annual meeting of the Association for Computational Linguistics*, ACL-44, pages 577–584, Stroudsburg, PA, USA. Association for Computational Linguistics.

A Cascaded Approach for Social Media Text Normalization of Turkish

Dilara Torunoğlu
Dep. of Computer Eng.
Istanbul Technical University
Istanbul, Turkey
torunoglud@itu.edu.tr

Gülşen Eryiğit
Dep. of Computer Eng.
Istanbul Technical University
Istanbul, Turkey
gulsen.cebiroglu@itu.edu.tr

Abstract

Text normalization is an indispensable stage for natural language processing of social media data with available NLP tools. We divide the normalization problem into 7 categories, namely; letter case transformation, replacement rules & lexicon lookup, proper noun detection, deasciification, vowel restoration, accent normalization and spelling correction. We propose a cascaded approach where each ill formed word passes from these 7 modules and is investigated for possible transformations. This paper presents the first results for the normalization of Turkish and tries to shed light on the different challenges in this area. We report a 40 percentage points improvement over a lexicon lookup baseline and nearly 50 percentage points over available spelling correctors.

1 Introduction

With the increasing number of people using micro blogging sites like Facebook and Twitter, social media became an indefinite source for machine learning area especially for natural language processing. This service is highly attractive for information extraction, text mining and opinion mining purposes as the large volumes of data available online daily. The language used in this platform differs severely from formally written text in that, people do not feel forced to write grammatically correct sentences, generally write like they talk or try to impress their thoughts within a limited number of characters (such as in Twitter 140 characters). This results with a totally different language than the conventional languages. The research on text normalization of social media gained speed towards the end of the last decade and as always, almost all of these elementary studies are conducted on the English language. We know from earlier research results that morphologically rich languages such as Turkish differ severely from English and the methods tailored for English do not fit for these languages. It is the case for text normalization as well.

Highly inflectional or agglutinative languages share the same characteristic that a unique lemma in these languages may have hundreds of possible surface forms. This increases the data sparsity in statistical models. For example, it's pointed out in Hakkani-Tür et al. (2000) that, it is due to Turkish language's inflectional and derivational morphology that the number of distinct word forms is very large compared to English distinct word size (Table 1). This large vocabulary size is the reason why the dictionary[1] lookup or similarity based approaches are not suitable for this kind of languages. And in addition to this, it is not an easy task to collect manually annotated data which could cover all these surface forms and their related mistakes for statistical approaches.

Corpus Size	Turkish	English
1M words	106,547	33,398
10M words	417,775	97,734

Table 1: Vocabulary sizes for two Turkish and English corpora (Hakkani-Tür et al., 2000)

In this paper, we propose a cascaded approach for the social text normalization (specifically for Tweets) of Turkish language. The approach is a combination of rule based and machine learning components for different layers of normalization, namely; letter case transformation, replacement rules & lexicon lookup, proper noun detection, deasciification, vowel restoration, accent normalization and spelling correction. Following the work of Han and Baldwin (2011), we divided the work into two stages: ill formed word detection

[1] For these languages, it is theoretically impossible to put every possible surface form into a dictionary.

and candidate word generation. Our contribution is: 1. a new normalization model which could be applied to other morphologically rich languages as well with appropriate NLP tools 2. the first results and test data sets for the text normalization of Turkish.

The paper is structured as follows: Section 2 and 3 give brief information about related work and morphologically rich languages, Section 4 presents our normalization approach and Section 5 the experimental setup, Section 6 gives our experimental results and discussions and Section 7 the conclusion.

2 Related Work

An important part of the previous studies have taken the normalization task either as a lexicon lookup (together with or without replacement rules) or as a statistical problem. There also exist many studies which use their combination. In these studies, a lexicon lookup is firstly employed for most common usage of slang words, abbreviations etc. and then a machine learning method is employed for the rest. Zhang et al. (2013) uses replacement rules and a graph based model in order to select the best rule combinations. Wang and Ng (2013) uses a beam search decoder. Hassan and Menezes (2013) propose an unsupervised approach which uses Random Walks on a contextual similarity bipartite graph constructed from n-gram sequences. In Han and Baldwin (2011), word similarity and context is used during lexicon lookup. Cook and Stevenson (2009) uses an unsupervised noisy channel model. Clark and Araki (2011) makes dictionary lookup. Liu et al. (2012) uses a unified letter transformation to generate possible ill formed words in order to use them in the training phase of a noisy channel model. Eisenstein (2013) analyzes phonological factors in social media writing.

Others, treating the normalization task as a machine translation (MT) problem which tries to translate from an ill formed language to a conventional one, form also another important group. For example the papers from Kaufmann and Kalita (2010), Pennell and Liu (2011), Aw et al. (2006) and Beaufort et al. (2010) may be collected under this group. Since the emergence of social media is very recent, only the latest studies are focused on this area and the earlier ones generally work for the text normalization in TTS (text-to-speech), ASR (automatic speech recognition) systems or SMS messages. Social media normalization poses new challenges on top of these, for example Twitter statuses contains mentions (@user_name), hashtags (#topic), variant number of emoticons (e.g. :) :@ <3 @>–) and special keywords (RT - retweet, DM - direct message etc.).

Although very rare, there are also some studies on languages other than English and these are mostly for speech recognition and SMS messages , e.g. Panchapagesan et al. (2004) for Hindi TTS, Nguyen et al. (2010) for Vietnamese TTS, Jia et al. (2008) for Mandarin TTS, Khan and Karim (2012) for Urdu SMS. To the best of our knowledge, our study is the first attempt for the normalization of social media data for morphologically rich languages.

3 Morphologically Rich Languages

Morphologically rich languages such as Turkish, Finnish, Korean, Hebrew etc., pose significant challenges for natural language processing tasks (Tsarfaty et al., 2013; Sarikaya et al., 2009). As stated previously, the highly productive morphology of these languages results in a very large number of word forms from a given stem. Table 2 lists only a few (among hundreds of possible) surface forms for the Turkish stem "ev" (*house*).

Surface form	English
ev	house
eve	to the house
evde	at the house
evdeki	(which is) at the house
evdekiler	those (who are) at the house
evdekilerde	at those (who are)

Table 2: Some surface forms for "ev" (*house*)

Sarikaya et al. (2009) list the emerging problems as below:

1. increase in dictionary size
2. poor language model probability estimation
3. higher out-of-vocabulary (OOV) rate
4. inflection gap for machine translation[2]

That is why, the normalization methods proposed so far (adapting MT or language models or

[2]Since, the number of possible word surface forms after inflections is very high, the alignment and translation accuracies in these languages are very badly affected.

lexicon lookup approaches) do not seem appropriate for the processing of morphologically rich languages, as in our case for Turkish.

4 The Proposed Architecture

We divide the normalization task into two parts: Ill-formed word detection and candidate generation. Figure 1 presents the architecture of the proposed normalization approach. The following subsections provide the details for both of these two parts and their components.

Before sending the input into these stages, we first use our tokenizer specifically tailored for Twitter for splitting the tweets into meaningful tokens. Our tokenizer is actually the first step of our normalization process since: 1. It intelligently splits the wrongly written word-punctuation combinations (e.g. "a,b" to [a , b]), while leaving "Ahmet'den" (*from Ahmet*) is left as it is since the apostrophe sign is used to append inflectional features to a proper noun.) 2. It does special processing for emoticons and consecutive punctuation marks so that they still reside together after the tokenization (e.g. :D or !!!!! are output as they occur).

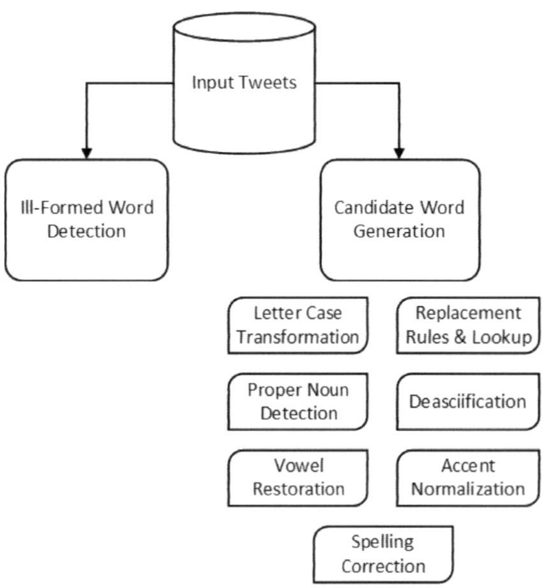

Figure 1: Normalization architecture

4.1 Ill-formed Word Detection

As stated earlier, since it is not possible to use a lexicon lookup table for morphologically rich languages, we use a morphological analyzer (Şahin et al., 2013) and an abbreviation list[3] and a list of 1045 abbreviations for controlling in-vocabulary (IV) words (labeled with a +NC "No Change" label for further use). By this way, we filter all the out-of-vocabulary (OOV) words and transfer them to the candidate generation process. Mentions (@user_name), hashtags (#topic), emoticons (:D), vocatives ("ahahahaha") and keywords ("RT") are also assumed to be OOV words since we want to detect these and tag them with special labels to be later used in higher-level NLP modules (e.g. POS tagging, syntactic analysis).

4.2 Candidate Generation

In the candidate generation part, we have seven components (rule based or machine learning models) which work sequentially. The outputs of each of these components are controlled by the morphological analyzer and if the normalized form from a component becomes an IV word then the process is terminated and the output is labeled with a relevant tag (provided in Table 3). Otherwise, the candidate generation process continues with the next component over the original input (except for the "Letter Case Transformation" and "Replacement Rules & Lexicon Lookup" components where the input is replaced by the modified output although it is still not an IV word, (see Section 4.2.1 and 4.2.2 for details).

Label	Component
+NC	No Change
+LCT	Letter Case Transformation
+RR	Replacement Rules & Lexicon Lookup
+PND	Proper Noun Detection
+DA	Deasciification
+VR	Vowel Restoration
+AN	Accent Normalization
+NoN	No Suggested Normalization

Table 3: Component Labels

4.2.1 Letter Case Transformation

An OOV token, coming to this stage, may be in one of the 4 different forms: lowercase, UPPERCASE, Proper Noun Case or miXEd CaSe. If the token is in lowercase and does not possess any specific punctuation marks for proper nouns (i.e. ' (apostrophe) or . (period)) , it is directly

[3] obtained from TLA (Turkish Language Association) http://www.tdk.gov.tr/index.php?option=com_content&id=198:Kisaltmalar

transferred to the next stage without any change (e.g. umuttan (*from hope*)). If the token is in Proper Noun Case (e.g. Umut'tan), it is accepted as a correct proper noun (even if it does not occur within the morphological analyzer's lexicon or was previously detected as an OOV word), left untouched (taking the label +NC) and excluded from all future evaluations.

For UPPERCASE, miXEd CaSe and lowercase words, we convert them into Proper Noun Case if they either contain an apostrophe (which is used in Turkish to separate inflectional suffixes from a proper noun) or a period (.) which is used formally in Turkish to denote abbreviations. These words are labeled with a "+LCT" label after the normalization. If the word does not contain any of these two marks, it is then converted into lowercase form and processed by the morphological analyzer as explained at the beginning of Section 4.2. It should be noted that all words going out from this component towards next stages are transformed into lowercase from this point on.

"ahmet'ten" – Proper Noun

"AHMET'TEN" – Proper Noun

"EACL."- Abbreviation

4.2.2 Replacement Rules & Lexicon Look-up

While normalizing the tweets, we have to deal with the following problems:

1. Slang words
2. Character repetition in interjections
3. Twitter-specific words
4. Emo style writing

We created a slang word lexicon of 272 words. This lexicon contains entries as the following: "kib" for "kendine iyi bak" (*take care of yourself*), "nbr" for "ne haber" (*what's up*). The tokens within the lexicon are directly replaced with their normalized forms.

Repetition of some characters within a word is a very common method to express exclamation in messages, such as in "lütfeeeennnn" instead of "lütfen" (*please*), "çoooooooook" instead of "çok" (*very*) and "ayyyyy" instead of "ay" (*oh!*). We reduce the repeated characters into a single character in the case that the consecutive occurrence count is greater than 2.

The usage of Twitter-specific words such as hashtags ("#topic"), mentions ("@user_name"), emoticons (":)"), vocatives ("hahahhah", "hööööö") and keywords ("RT") also causes a host of problems. The recurring patterns in vocatives are reduced into minimal forms during the normalization process, as for "haha" instead of "hahahhah" and "hö" instead of "hööööö".

Emo style writing, as in the example "$eker 4you" instead of "şeker senin için" (*sweety, it's for you*), is another problematic field for the normalization task. We created 35 replacement rules with regular expressions in order to automatically correct or label the given input for Twitter-specific words and Emo style writing. Examples include "$ → ş", "ϵ → e", "3 → e" and "!→ i". Through these replacement rules, we are able to correct most instances of Emo style writing.

Our regular expressions also label the following token types by the given specific labels for future reference:

- **Mentions:** Nicknames that refer to users on Twitter are labeled as e.g. *@mention[@dida]*
- **Hashtags:** Hashtags that refer to trending topics on Twitter are labeled as e.g. *@hashtag[#geziparki]*
- **Vocatives:** Vocatives are labeled as e.g. *@vocative[hehe]*
- **Smileys:** Emoticons are labeled as e.g. *@smiley[:)]*
- **Twitter-specific Keywords:** Keywords like "RT", "DM", "MT", "Reply" etc. are labeled as e.g. *@keyword[RT]*

Figure 2 shows the normalized version of a tweet in informal Turkish that could be translated like "*@dida what's up, why don't you call #offended :(*", before and after being processed by this component. Although the word "aramıon" also needs normalization as "aramıyorsun" (*you don't call*), this transformation is not realized within the current component and applied later in the accent normalization component given in Section 4.2.6.

4.2.3 Proper Noun Detection

As previously stated, all OOV words coming to this stage are in lowercase. In this component, our aim is to detect proper nouns erroneously written in lowercase (such as "ahmetten" or "ahmetden") and convert them to proper noun case with correct formatting ("Ahmet'ten" for the aforementioned examples).

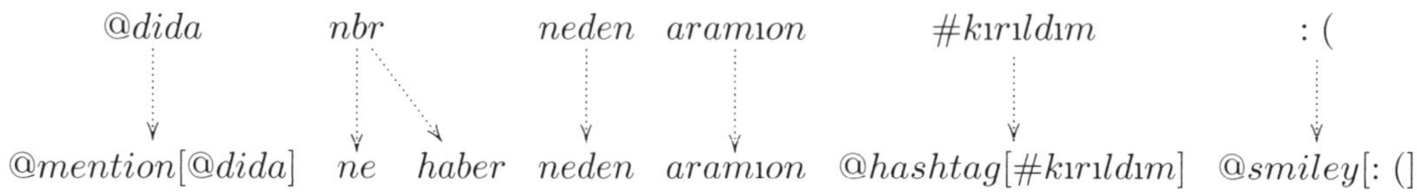

Figure 2: Normalization with Replacement Rules & Lexicon Look-up

For this purpose, we use proper name gazetteers from Şeker and Eryiğit (2012) together with a newly added organization gazetteer of 122 tokens in order to check whether a given word could be a proper noun. Turkish proper nouns are very frequently selected from common nouns such as "Çiçek" (*flower*), "Şeker" (*sugar*) and "İpek" (*silk*). Therefore, it is quite difficult to recognize such words as proper nouns when they are written in lowercase, as the task could not be accomplished by just checking the existence of such words within the gazetteers.

For our proper noun detection component, we use the below strategy:
1. We reduce the size of the gazetteers by removing all words with length ≤ 2 characters, or with a ratio value under our specified threshold (1.5). Ratio value is calculated, according to the formula given in Equation 1, considering the occurrence counts from two big corpora, the METU-Sabancı Treebank (Say et al., 2002) and the web corpus of Sak et al. (2011). Table 4 gives the counts for three sample words. One may observe from the table that "ahmet" occured 40 times in proper case and 20 times in lower case form within the two corpora resulting in a ratio value of 2.0. Since the ratio value for "umut" is only 0.4 (which is under our threshold), this noun is removed from our gazetteers so that it would not be transformed into proper case in case it is found to occur in lowercase form. A similar case holds for the word "sağlam" (healthy). Although it is a very frequent Turkish family name, it is observed in our corpora mostly as a common noun with a ratio value of 0.09.

$$ratio(w_n) = \frac{Occurence\_in\_Propercase(w_n)}{Occurence\_in\_Lowercase(w_n)} \quad (1)$$

2. We pass the tokens to a morphological analyzer for unknown words (Şahin et al., 2013) and find possible lemmata as in the example below. We then search for the longest possible stem within our gazetteers (e.g. the longest stem for "ahmetten" found within the name gazetteer is "ahmet"), and when a stem is found within the gazetteers, the initial letter of the stem is capitalized and the inflectional suffixes after the stem are separated by use of an apostrophe ("Ahmet'ten"). If none of the possible stems is found within the gazetteers, the word is left as is and transferred to the next stage in its original form.

Proper Case	Lowercase	Sense	Ratio
Sağlam=9	sağlam=100	healthy	Ratio=0.09
Umut=40	umut=100	hope	Ratio=0.4
Ahmet=40	ahmet=20	n/a	Ratio=2.0

Table 4: Example of Ratio Values

"ahmet +Noun+A3sg+Pnon+Abl"

"ahmette +Noun+A3sg+Pnom+Loc"

"ahmetten +Noun+A3sg+Pnon+Nom"

4.2.4 Deasciification

The role of the deasciifier is the reconstruction of Turkish-specific characters with diacritics (i.e. ı, İ, ş, ö, ç, ğ, ü) from their ASCII-compliant counterparts (i.e. i, I, s, o, c, g, u). Most users of social media use asciified letters, which should be corrected in order to obtain valid Turkish words. The task is also not straightforward because of the ambiguity potential in asciified forms, as between the words "yasa" (*law*) and "yaşa" (*live*). For this stage, we use the deasciifier of Yüret (Yüret and de la Maza, 2006) which implements the GPA algorithm (which itself is basically a decision tree implementation) in order to produce the most likely deasciified form of the input.

4.2.5 Vowel Restoration

There is a new trend of omitting vowels in typing among the Turkish social media users, in order to reduce the message length. In this stage, we process tokens written with consonants only (e.g. "svyrm"), which is how vowel omission often happens. The aim of the vowel restoration is the generation of the original word by adding vowels into the appropriate places (e.g. "svyrm" to "seviyorum" (*I love*)). We employed a vocalizer (Adalı and Eryiğit, 2014) which uses CRFs for the construction of the most probable vocalized output.

4.2.6 Accent Normalization

In the social media platform, people generally write like they talk by transferring the pronounced versions of the words directly to the written text. Eisenstein (2013) also discusses the situation for the English case. In the accent normalization module we are trying to normalize this kind of writings into proper forms. Some examples are given below:

"gidicem" instead of "gideceğim"

(I'll go)

"geliyonmu?" instead of "geliyor musun?"

(Are you coming?)

In this component, we first try to detect the most common verb accents (generally endings such as "-cem, -yom, -çaz" etc.) used in social media and then uses regular expression rules in order to replace these endings with their equivalent morphological analysis. One should note that since in most of the morphologically rich languages, the verb also carries inflections related to the person agreement, we produce rules for catching all the possible surface forms of these accents.

Table 5 introduces some of these replacement rules (column 1 and column 3). As a result, the word "gidcem" becomes "git+Verb+Pos+Fut+A1sg"[4]. We then use a morphological generator and takes the corrected output (if any) "gideceğim" *(I'll go)* for "git+Verb+Pos+Fut+A1sg"[5].

We also have more complex replacement rules in order to process more complex accent problems. To give an example, the proper form of the word "gidiyonmu" is actually "gidiyor musun" *(are you going)* and in the formal form it is the question enclitic ("mu") which takes the person agreement ("-sun" 2. person singular) where as in the accent form the person agreement appears before "mu" as a single letter "gidiyo**n**mu".

[4]Please note that, we also change the last letter of the stem according to the harmonization rules of Turkish: the last letters "bcdg" are changed to "pçtk".

[5]the morphological tags in the table stands for: *+Pos*: Positive, *+Prog1*: Present continuous tense, *+A2sg*: 2. person singular, *+Fut*: Future tense, *+A1sg*: 1. person singular, *+A1pl*: 1. person plural

Accent endings	Correct endings	Morph. Analysis
+iyon	+iyorsun	+Verb+Pos+Prog1+A2sg
+cem	+eceğim	+Verb+Pos+Fut+A1sg
+caz	+acağız	+Verb+Pos+Fut+A1pl

Table 5: Accent Normalization Replacement Rules

4.2.7 Spelling Correction

As the last component of our normalization approach, we propose to use a high performance spelling corrector. This spelling corrector should especially give a high precision score rather than recall since the false positives have a very harming effect on the normalization task by producing outputs with a totally different meaning. Unfortunately, we could not find such a corrector for Turkish. We tested with an MsWord plugin and the spelling corrector of Zemberek (Akın and Akın, 2007) and obtained a negative impact by using both. We are planning to create such a spelling corrector as future work.

If an OOV word couldn't still be normalized at the end of the proposed iterative model (consisting 7 components), it is labeled with a "+NoN" label and left in its original input format.

5 Experimental Setup

In this section we provide information about our used data sets, our evaluation strategy and the used models in the experiments.

5.1 Data Sets

To test our success rates, we used a total of 1,200 tweets aligned and normalized manually. The manual alignment is a one-to-many token alignment task from the original input towards the normalized forms. To give an example, the slang usage "kib" will be aligned to 3 tokens ("kendine iyi bak" *(take care of yourself)*) on the normalized tweet. Although there are cases for many-to-one alignment (such as in "cats,dogs"), these are handled in the tokenization stage before the normalization. We used half of this data set as our validation set during the development of our proposed components and reserved the remaining 600 tweets (collected from a different time slot) as a totally unseen data set for using at the end. Table 6 provides some statistics over these data sets: the number of tweets, the number of tokens and the

Data Sets	# Tweets	# Tokens	# OOV
Validation Set	600	6,322	2,708
Test Set	600	7,061	2,192

Table 6: Description of the Data Sets

number of OOV tokens.

Besides the aforementioned datasets, we also had access to a much bigger Twitter data set consisting of 4,049 manually normalized tweets (Eryiğit et al., 2013) (59,012 tokens in total). The only difference of this data set is that the tweets are not aligned on token level as in the previously introduced data sets. That is why, it is not possible to use them for gold standard evaluation of our system. But in order to be able to have an idea about the performance of the previous approaches regarding lexicon lookup, we decided to automatically align this set and create a baseline lexicon lookup model for comparison purposes. (see the details in Section 5.3).

5.2 Evaluation Method

We evaluated our work both for ill formed word detection and candidate generation separately. For ill formed word detection, we provide precision (P), recall (R), f-measure (F) and accuracy (Acc.) scores. For candidate generation, we provide only the accuracy scores (the number of correctly normalized tokens over the total number of detected ill formed words).

5.3 Compared Models

To the best of our knowledge this study is the first attempt for the normalization of Turkish social media data. Since there are only spelling corrector systems available for the task we compared the proposed model with them. In other words, we compared 3 different models with our proposed system:

Model 1 (MsWord) is the model where we use an api for getting the MsWord Turkish spelling suggestions. Although this is not a tool developed for normalization purposes we wanted to see its success on our data sets. We accepted the top best suggestion as the normalized version for the input tokens.

Model 2 (Zemberek) (Akın and Akın, 2007) is also an open source spelling corrector for Turkish.

Model 3 (Lookup Table) is a model that we developed with the aim of creating a baseline lookup approach for comparison. For this purpose, we first used GIZA++ (Och and Ney, 2000) in order to automatically align the normalized tweets (using the 4,049 tweets' data set presented in Section 5.1) and created a lookup table with the produced aligned token sequences. We then used this lookup table to check for the existence of each ill formed word and get its normalized counterpart.

6 Experimental Results

Table 7 and Table 8 gives the results of the ill formed word detection for different systems for the validation set and the test set consecutively. In these experiments, we do not provide the results of the "Lookup Table" model since the ill formed detection part of it is exactly the same with our proposed model. For MsWord and Zemberek we considered each modified word as an ill formed word detected by that system. We can see from the tables that our proposed model has an f-measure of ill formed word detection 0.78. As it is explained in Section 4.1, our ill formed word detection approach is very straightforward and it uses only a morphological analyzer and an abbreviation list in order to detect OOV words. Thus, one may wonder why the scores for the proposed model are not very close to 1 although it outperforms all of its available rivals. This is because, there exists nearly 20% of the ill formed tokens which are not suspended to our morphological filter although they are manually annotated as ill formed by human annotators. This is certainly possible for morphologically rich languages since a word surface form may be the valid analysis of many stems. The ill formed word "çalışıcım" is a good example for this situation. Although this word will be understood by most of the people as the ill formed version of the word "çalışacağım" (*I'm going to work*), it is considered by the morphological analyzer as a valid Turkish word since although very rare, it could also be the surface form of the word "çalış" with additional derivational and inflectional suffixes "çalış+ıcı+m" meaning "*my worker*".

Systems	P	R	F	Acc.
MsWord	0.25	0.59	0.35	0.58
Zemberek	0.21	0.17	0.19	0.21
Proposed Model	0.75	0.81	0.78	0.80

Table 7: Ill Formed Word Detection Evaluation Results on Validation Set

Systems	P	R	F	Acc.
MsWord	0.24	0.19	0.21	0.56
Zemberek	0.11	0.29	0.20	0.11
Proposed Model	0.71	0.72	0.71	0.86

Table 8: Ill Formed Word Detection Evaluation Results on Test Set

Data Set	Systems	Accuracy
Validation Set	MsWord	0.25
	Zemberek	0.21
	Lookup Table	0.34
	Proposed Model	0.75
Test Set	MsWord	0.24
	Zemberek	0.11
	Lookup Table	0.31
	Proposed Model	0.71

Table 9: Candidate Generation Results on Data Sets

Table 9 gives the evaluation scores of each different system for both the validation and test data sets. Although the lookup model is very basic, one can observe from the table that it outperforms both MsWord and Zemberek. Our proposed iterative model obtains the highest scores (75% for validation and 71% for test sets) with a relative improvement of 40 percentage points over the lexicon lookup baseline.

7 Conclusion

In this paper we presented a cascaded normalization model for Turkish which could also be applied to the morphologically rich languages with appropriate NLP tools. The model has two main parts: ill formed word detection and candidate word generation consisting of 7 normalization stages (letter case transformation, replacement rules & lexicon lookup, proper noun detection, deasciification, vowel restoration, accent normalization and spelling correction) executed sequentially one on top of the other one. We present the first and highest results for Turkish text normalization[6] of social media data with a 86% accuracy of ill formed word detection and 71% accuracy for candidate word generation. A morphological analyzer is used for the detection of ill formed words. But we believe the accuracy of this first detection stage may be improved by the addition of a lexicon lookup (before the morphological filter) consisting the most frequent normalization cases extracted from manually normalized data if available. Thus, as a future work we plan to extend our work both on the ill formed word detection and on the creation of a spelling corrector with social web data in focus.

[6]The produced test sets and the Web interface of the Turkish Normalizer is available via http://tools.nlp.itu.edu.tr (Eryiğit, 2014)

Acknowledgment

This work is part of our ongoing research project "Parsing Turkish Web 2.0 Sentences" supported by ICT COST Action IC1207 TUBITAK 1001 (grant no: 112E276). The authors want to thank Turkcell Global Bilgi for sharing the manually normalized data of user comments from the Telecom domain. We also want to thank Ozan Arkan Can for his valuable discussions and helps during the data preparation.

References

Kübra Adalı and Gülşen Eryiğit. 2014. Vowel and diacritic restoration for social media texts. In *5th Workshop on Language Analysis for Social Media (LASM) at EACL*, Gothenburg, Sweden, April. Association for Computational Linguistics.

Ahmet Afsin Akın and Mehmet Dündar Akın. 2007. Zemberek, an open source nlp framework for turkic languages. *Structure*.

AiTi Aw, Min Zhang, Juan Xiao, and Jian Su. 2006. A phrase-based statistical model for sms text normalization. In *Proc. of the COLING/ACL on Main conference poster sessions*, COLING-ACL '06, pages 33–40, Stroudsburg, PA, USA. Association for Computational Linguistics.

Richard Beaufort, Sophie Roekhaut, Louise-Amélie Cougnon, and Cédrick Fairon. 2010. A hybrid rule/model-based finite-state framework for normalizing sms messages. In *Proc. of the 48th Annual Meeting of the Association for Computational Linguistics*, ACL '10, pages 770–779, Stroudsburg, PA, USA. Association for Computational Linguistics.

Eleanor Clark and Kenji Araki. 2011. Text normalization in social media: progress, problems and applications for a pre-processing system of casual english. *Procedia-Social and Behavioral Sciences*, 27:2–11.

Paul Cook and Suzanne Stevenson. 2009. An unsupervised model for text message normalization. In *Proc. of the Workshop on Computational Approaches to Linguistic Creativity*, CALC '09, pages 71–78, Stroudsburg, PA, USA. Association for Computational Linguistics.

Jacob Eisenstein. 2013. Phonological factors in social media writing. In *Proc. of the Workshop on Language Analysis in Social Media*, pages 11–19, Atlanta, Georgia, June. Association for Computational Linguistics.

Gülşen Eryiğit, Fatih Samet Çetin, Meltem Yanık, Tanel Temel, and İyas Çiçekli. 2013. Turksent: A sentiment annotation tool for social media. In *Proc. of the 7th Linguistic Annotation Workshop and Interoperability with Discourse*, pages 131–134, Sofia, Bulgaria, August. Association for Computational Linguistics.

Gülşen Eryiğit. 2014. ITU Turkish NLP web service. In *Proc. of the Demonstrations at the 14th Conference of the European Chapter of the Association for Computational Linguistics (EACL)*, Gothenburg, Sweden, April. Association for Computational Linguistics.

Dilek Z. Hakkani-Tür, Kemal Oflazer, and Gökhan Tür. 2000. Statistical morphological disambiguation for agglutinative languages. In *Proc. of the 18th conference on Computational linguistics - Volume 1*, COLING '00, pages 285–291, Stroudsburg, PA, USA. Association for Computational Linguistics.

Bo Han and Timothy Baldwin. 2011. Lexical normalisation of short text messages: Makn sens a #twitter. In *Proc. of the 49th ACL HLT*, pages 368–378, Portland, Oregon, USA, June. Association for Computational Linguistics.

Hany Hassan and Arul Menezes. 2013. Social text normalization using contextual graph random walks. In *Proc. of the 51st ACL*, pages 1577–1586, Sofia, Bulgaria, August. Association for Computational Linguistics.

Yuxiang Jia, Dezhi Huang, Wu Liu, Shiwen Yu, and Haila Wang. 2008. Text normalization in Mandarin text-to-speech system. In *ICASSP*, pages 4693–4696. IEEE.

Max Kaufmann and Jugal Kalita. 2010. Syntactic normalization of Twitter messages. In *Proc. of the 8th International Conference on Natural Language Processing (ICON 2010)*, Chennai, India. Macmillan India.

Osama A Khan and Asim Karim. 2012. A rule-based model for normalization of sms text. In *Tools with Artificial Intelligence (ICTAI), 2012 IEEE 24th International Conference on*, volume 1, pages 634–641. IEEE.

Fei Liu, Fuliang Weng, and Xiao Jiang. 2012. A broad-coverage normalization system for social media language. In *Proc. of the 50th ACL*, pages 1035–1044, Stroudsburg, PA, USA. Association for Computational Linguistics.

Thu-Trang Thi Nguyen, Thanh Thi Pham, and Do-Dat Tran. 2010. A method for vietnamese text normalization to improve the quality of speech synthesis. In *Proc. of the 2010 Symposium on Information and Communication Technology*, SoICT '10, pages 78–85, New York, NY, USA. ACM.

Franz Josef Och and Hermann Ney. 2000. Giza++: Training of statistical translation models.

K Panchapagesan, Partha Pratim Talukdar, N Sridhar Krishna, Kalika Bali, and AG Ramakrishnan. 2004. Hindi text normalization. In *Fifth International Conference on Knowledge Based Computer Systems (KBCS)*, pages 19–22. Citeseer.

Deana Pennell and Yang Liu. 2011. A character-level machine translation approach for normalization of sms abbreviations. In *IJCNLP*, pages 974–982.

Muhammet Şahin, Umut Sulubacak, and Gülşen Eryiğit. 2013. Redefinition of turkish morphology using flag diacritics. In *Proc. of The Tenth Symposium on Natural Language Processing (SNLP-2013)*, Phuket, Thailand, October.

Haşim Sak, Tunga Güngör, and Murat Saraçlar. 2011. Resources for Turkish morphological processing. *Lang. Resour. Eval.*, 45(2):249–261, May.

Ruhi Sarikaya, Katrin Kirchhoff, Tanja Schultz, and Dilek Hakkani-Tur. 2009. Introduction to the special issue on processing morphologically rich languages. *Trans. Audio, Speech and Lang. Proc.*, 17(5):861–862, July.

Bilge Say, Deniz Zeyrek, Kemal Oflazer, and Umut Özge. 2002. Development of a corpus and a treebank for present-day written Turkish. In *Proc. of the Eleventh International Conference of Turkish Linguistics*, Famaguste, Cyprus, August.

Gökhan Akın Şeker and Gülşen Eryiğit. 2012. Initial explorations on using CRFs for Turkish named entity recognition. In *Proc. of COLING 2012*, Mumbai, India, 8-15 December.

Reut Tsarfaty, Djamé Seddah, Sandra Kübler, and Joakim Nivre. 2013. Parsing morphologically rich languages: Introduction to the special issue. *Computational Linguistics*, 39(1):15–22.

Pidong Wang and Hwee Tou Ng. 2013. A beam-search decoder for normalization of social media text with application to machine translation. In *Proc. of NAACL-HLT*, pages 471–481.

Deniz Yüret and Michael de la Maza. 2006. The greedy prepend algorithm for decision list induction. In *Proc. of the 21st international conference on Computer and Information Sciences*, ISCIS'06, pages 37–46, Berlin, Heidelberg. Springer-Verlag.

Congle Zhang, Tyler Baldwin, Howard Ho, Benny Kimelfeld, and Yunyao Li. 2013. Adaptive parser-centric text normalization. In *Proc. of the 51st ACL*, pages 1159–1168, Sofia, Bulgaria, August. Association for Computational Linguistics.

Experiments to Improve Named Entity Recognition on Turkish Tweets

Dilek Küçük and **Ralf Steinberger**
European Commission, Joint Research Centre
Via E. Fermi 2749
21027 Ispra (VA), Italy
firstname.lastname@jrc.ec.europa.eu

Abstract

Social media texts are significant information sources for several application areas including trend analysis, event monitoring, and opinion mining. Unfortunately, existing solutions for tasks such as named entity recognition that perform well on formal texts usually perform poorly when applied to social media texts. In this paper, we report on experiments that have the purpose of improving named entity recognition on Turkish tweets, using two different annotated data sets. In these experiments, starting with a baseline named entity recognition system, we adapt its recognition rules and resources to better fit Twitter language by relaxing its capitalization constraint and by diacritics-based expansion of its lexical resources, and we employ a simplistic normalization scheme on tweets to observe the effects of these on the overall named entity recognition performance on Turkish tweets. The evaluation results of the system with these different settings are provided with discussions of these results.

1 Introduction

Analysis of social media texts, particularly microblog texts like tweets, has attracted recent attention due to significance of the contained information for diverse application areas like trend analysis, event monitoring, and opinion mining. Tools for well-studied problems like named entity recognition (NER) are usually employed as components within these social media analysis applications. For instance, in (Abel et al., 2011), named entities extracted from tweets are used to determine trending topics for user modeling within the context of personalized recommender systems and in (Ritter et al., 2012), named entities in tweets are used to complement the events extracted by an open domain event extraction system for Twitter. However, existing NER solutions for well-formed text types like news articles are reported to suffer from considerable performance degradations when they are ported to social media texts, mainly due to the peculiarities of this latter text type (Ritter et al., 2011).

In this paper, we report on our NER experiments on Turkish tweets in order to determine facilitating and impeding factors during the development of a NER system for Turkish tweets which can be used in social media analysis applications. We carry out these experiments on two tweet data sets annotated with named entities. After the initial evaluation results of a rule-based NER system (Küçük and Yazıcı, 2009) on these data sets, we gradually present the performance results achieved by the extended versions of the system together with discussions of these results. For these experiments, we first perform two system adaptations, i.e., relaxing the capitalization constraint of the system and diacritics-based expansion of the system's lexical resources. Next, we incorporate a simplistic tweet normalization scheme into the NER procedure. After the evaluation of these extensions, we provide discussions on the plausible features of a NER system tailored to Turkish tweets.

The rest of the paper is organized as follows: In Section 2, we review the literature on NER on tweets and NER on Turkish texts. In Section 3, we present our NER experiments on Turkish tweets. Directions of future work are outlined in Section 4 and finally Section 5 concludes the paper.

2 Related Work

There are several recent studies presenting approaches for NER on microblog texts, especially on tweets in English. Among these studies, in (Ritter et al., 2011), a NER system tailored to tweets, called T-NER, is presented which employs Conditional Random Fields (CRF) for named entity segmentation and labelled topic modelling for subsequent classification, using Freebase dictionaries. A hybrid approach to NER on tweets is presented in (Liu et al., 2011) where k-Nearest Neighbor and CRF based classifiers are sequentially applied. In (Liu et al., 2012), a factor graph based approach is proposed that jointly performs NER and named entity normalization on tweets. An unsupervised approach that performs only named entity extraction on tweets using resources like Wikipedia is described in (Li et al., 2012). A clustering-based approach for NER on microtexts is presented in (Jung, 2012), a lightweight filter based approach for NER on tweets is described in (de Oliveira et al., 2013), and a series of NER experiments on targeted tweets in Polish is presented in (Piskorski and Ehrmann, 2013). Finally, an adaptation of the ANNIE component of GATE framework to microblog texts, called TwitIE, is described in (Bontcheva et al., 2013).

Considering NER research on Turkish texts, various approaches have been employed so far including those based on using Hidden Markov Models (HMM) (Tür et al., 2003), on manually engineered recognition rules (Küçük and Yazıcı, 2009; Küçük and Yazıcı, 2012), on rule learning (Tatar and Çicekli, 2011), and on CRFs (Yeniterzi, 2011; Şeker and Eryiğit, 2012). All of these approaches have been proposed for news texts and the CRF-based approach (Şeker and Eryiğit, 2012) is reported to outperform the previous proposals with a balanced F-Measure of about 91%.

To the best of our knowledge, there are only two studies on NER from Turkish tweets. In (Çelikkaya et al., 2013), the CRF-based NER system (Şeker and Eryiğit, 2012) is evaluated on informal text types and is reported to achieve an F-Measure of 19% on tweets. In (Küçük et al., 2014), a tweet data set in Turkish annotated with named entities is presented. The adaptation of a multilingual rule-based NER system (Pouliquen and Steinberger, 2009) to Turkish, which achieves an F-Measure of about 61% on a news article data set, gets an F-Measure of 37% on this tweet data set, and after extending the resources of the NER system with frequently appearing person and organization names in Turkish news articles, the corresponding scores increase to about 69% and 43%, respectively (Küçük et al., 2014).

Table 1: NE Statistics on the Data Sets.

	Frequency in	
NE Type	**Tweet Set-1**	**Tweet Set-2**
Person	457	774
Location	282	191
Organization	241	409
All PLOs	980	1,374
Date	201	342
Time	5	25
Money	16	13
Percent	9	3
All NEs	1,211	1,757

3 Named Entity Recognition Experiments

The NER experiments are performed using the rule-based NER system (Küçük and Yazıcı, 2009) which makes use of a set of lexical resources, i.e., lists of person/location/organization names (henceforth referred to as PLOs), and patterns for the extraction of named entities (NEs) of type PLOs and time/date/money/percent expressions (Küçük and Yazıcı, 2009). The system is proposed for news articles which is a considerably well-formed text type usually with proper capitalization of the initial letters of PLOs and separation of these PLOs from their suffixes with apostrophes[1]. Yet, as even such well-formed texts may be lacking these important indicators of PLOs, the system can be configured to make use of the capitalization clue or not, and it includes a simplistic morphological analyzer to check the suffixes at the end of PLO candidates and thereby validate these candidates (Küçük and Yazıcı, 2009).

This NER system achieves a balanced F-Measure of 78.7% (without giving any credit to partial extractions) on a news article data set of about 20K tokens obtained from the METU Turkish corpus (Say et al., 2002) where the annotated form of this data set includes a total of 1,613 NEs. Within the course of the current study, we have evaluated this system on two tweet data sets in Turkish where statistical information about these data sets are provided in Table 1. The first one, which is referred to as $Tweet\ Set{-}1$ in Table 1, is presented in (Küçük et al., 2014) and comprises 2,320 tweets with about 20K tokens. The second data set ($Tweet\ Set{-}2$) includes about 5K

[1] An example inflected named entity of location name type (a city name) in Turkish which takes the dative case suffix ($-ya$) is $Ankara'ya$ (meaning $to\ Ankara$) where the initial letter of the named entity is properly capitalized and the case suffix is accordingly separated from the entity with an apostrophe.

tweets with about 50K tokens and is described in (Çelikkaya et al., 2013).

3.1 Initial Experiments

We have first evaluated the system's performance on the data sets without any extensions to the existing NER system. Table 2 presents these evaluation results using the commonly employed metrics of precision, recall, and balanced F-Measure, without giving any credit to partially extracted NEs. Table 3 displays those results with the same metrics this time giving credit to partial extractions with the constraint that the NE type within the system output and the answer key must be the same, where these metrics have been employed in studies like (Maynard et al., 2001).

The evaluation results in Table 2 and Table 3 are in line with the common finding reported in the literature that the NER systems for comparatively well-formed text types face considerable performance decreases when they are evaluated on tweets. This observation is usually attributed to the peculiarities of tweet texts such as common grammatical/spelling errors and deliberate contractions. With strict metrics, the system is reported to achieve an F-Measure rate of 78.7%. When it is ported to tweets, the best overall F-Measure rates achieved are 53.23% and 44.25% on $Tweet\ Set{-}1$ and $Tweet\ Set{-}2$, respectively, while the corresponding best F-Measure rates for only PLOs are 47.76% and 36.63%, respectively, all with strict metrics. The difference between the results for PLOs and the overall results also confirms that the system recognizes temporal and numerical expressions (within its scope) with decent performance, compared to the recognition of PLOs.

The F-Measure rates obtained when partial extractions are also given credit are about 5% higher than those obtained without giving any credit to partially extracted NEs. This increase is important due to pragmatic reasons as these partially extracted NEs can help conveniently filter tweet streams and retrieve relevant subsets of tweets in several application settings.

3.2 NER Experiments with Rule/Resource Adaptations

Tweet texts possess the following peculiarities usually as opposed to other formal text types:

- Grammatical/spelling errors are common, like incorrectly writing proper names all in lowercase letters. A Turkish example illustrating a spelling error is the use of $geliyoooo$ instead of $geliyor$ (meaning $is\ coming$).
- Contracted word forms are commonly used instead of full forms, like referring to the football club called $Fenerbahçe$ as $Fener$ only, where the latter contracted form is also homonymous to a common name in Turkish (meaning $lantern$).
- For the particular case of Turkish tweets, non-accentuated characters (c, g, i, o, s, and u) are often utilized instead of the corresponding Turkish characters with diacritics (ç, ğ, ı, ö, ş, and ü). An example of this phenomenon is writing $cunku$ instead of the correct form, *çünkü* (meaning $because$).

Considering the above features, in order to improve the initial NER performance on Turkish tweets, we have tested two adaptations of the rule-based NER system. The details of these adaptations and the corresponding evaluation results are presented in the following subsections.

3.2.1 Relaxing the Capitalization Constraint of the System

As proper capitalization of PLOs is usually lacking in tweets, we have evaluated the NER system with its capitalization feature turned off, so that the system considers all tokens (no matter whether their initial character is capitalized or not) as valid NE candidates. The initial evaluation results of the system with this setting are provided in Table 2 and Table 3 within the rows where the $Capitalization$ column has a corresponding OFF value. The results for these two capitalization settings are also similarly provided in Tables 4-6 which present the evaluation results described in the upcoming sections.

The results in Table 2 and Table 3 demonstrate that relaxing the capitalization constraint (i.e., not using the capitalization clue) during the NER procedure on Turkish tweets consistently improves performance for PLOs on both data sets. The improvement obtained with this relaxation is more dramatic on $Tweet\ Set{-}2$ and for this data set the overall results are accordingly better than those obtained when the capitalization clue is used. It should again be noted that the NER system uses a

Table 2: Initial NER Evaluation Results (Strict Metrics).

Data Set	Capitalization	Metric	Person	Location	Organization	Overall for PLOs	Overall for 7 Types
Tweet Set-1	ON	P (%)	52.82	77.78	72.34	64.16	71.13
		R (%)	32.82	49.65	28.22	36.53	42.53
		F (%)	**40.49**	**60.61**	**40.60**	**46.55**	**53.23**
	OFF	P (%)	36.73	71.72	58.70	49.29	56.21
		R (%)	43.33	62.06	33.61	46.33	50.45
		F (%)	**39.76**	**66.54**	**42.74**	**47.76**	**53.18**
Tweet Set-2	ON	P (%)	55.79	58.68	72.06	58.86	65.62
		R (%)	20.54	37.17	11.98	20.31	30.85
		F (%)	**30.03**	**45.51**	**20.55**	**30.19**	**41.97**
	OFF	P (%)	35.61	45.53	40.72	38.31	46.27
		R (%)	38.37	61.26	16.63	35.08	42.40
		F (%)	**36.94**	**52.23**	**23.61**	**36.63**	**44.25**

Table 3: Initial NER Evaluation Results (Partial Metrics).

Data Set	Capitalization	Metric	Person	Location	Organization	Overall for PLOs	Overall for 7 Types
Tweet Set-1	ON	P (%)	65.33	86.05	88.37	75.98	80.74
		R (%)	39.38	54.01	32.34	41.87	47.13
		F (%)	**49.14**	**66.37**	**47.35**	**53.99**	**59.52**
	OFF	P (%)	42.83	78.68	69.11	56.25	62.49
		R (%)	50.92	67.71	38.00	52.55	55.72
		F (%)	**46.53**	**72.78**	**49.04**	**54.34**	**58.91**
Tweet Set-2	ON	P (%)	69.79	61.34	74.63	68.27	72.51
		R (%)	24.28	38.62	12.25	22.65	33.31
		F (%)	**36.03**	**47.40**	**21.05**	**34.02**	**45.65**
	OFF	P (%)	41.82	48.41	41.99	43.21	50.91
		R (%)	45.10	65.59	17.06	39.38	46.45
		F (%)	**43.40**	**55.71**	**24.26**	**41.21**	**48.58**

simplistic morphological analyzer to validate suffixes added at the ends of the NEs, thereby the system does not overgenerate with this new setting, although the precision rates decrease considerably in return to corresponding increases in the recall rates. To summarize, together with the fact that about 25.1% of all PLOs within $Tweet\ Set{-}1$ are lacking proper capitalization (Küçük et al., 2014), these findings suggest that the ability to relax this capitalization constraint is a convenient feature of a practical NER system for Turkish tweets. An alternative feature would be to automatically correct the capitalization of NEs instead, as a preprocessing step.

3.2.2 Diacritics-Based Expansion of the Lexical Resources

In Turkish tweet texts, words including Turkish characters with diacritics are often, usually either erroneously or deliberately for pragmatic reasons such as to type faster, spelled with their non-diacritic equivalents, as pointed out above. Therefore, we expand the entries in the lexical resources of the NER system to include both diacritic and non-diacritic variants of these entries. For instance, the Turkish name of the island $Cyprus$, $Kıbrıs$, may appear in tweets as $Kıbris$, $Kibrıs$, or $Kibris$, as well. As this example denotes, for each existing entry with n such Turkish-specific characters, 2^n entries (including the original entry) are included in the ultimate expanded forms of the lexical resources, since each such character may be used as it is or may be replaced with its equivalent.

During this expansion stage, we have applied a filtering procedure over these newly considered $2^n - 1$ entries to check whether they are homonymous to common names in Turkish. This filtering procedure basically checks whether an expansion candidate is within a list of unique, supposedly well-formed, Turkish words comprising about 1,140,208 items including inflected forms (Zemberek, 2010), and if it is, then this candidate is discarded to avoid overgeneration during the actual NER procedure.

We have tested this new version of the system with expanded lexical resources and the corresponding evaluation results are provided in Table 4 and Table 5, using the strict and partial evaluation metrics, respectively. Both strict and partial evaluation results denote that the performance of the system is improved after this diacritics-based expansion of the system resources. The best results are obtained when this expansion is combined with the relaxation of the capitalization constraint, for PLOs on $Tweet\ Set{-}1$, and both for PLOs and all 7 NE types on $Tweet\ Set{-}2$. Similar to the points made in the previous section, this diacritics-based expansion scheme stands as a promising feature of an ultimate NER system for Turkish tweets, also considering the fact that

Table 4: NER Evaluation Results After Diacritics-Based Expansion of Resources (Strict Metrics).

Data Set	Capitalization	Metric	Person	Location	Organization	Overall for PLOs	Overall for 7 Types
Tweet Set-1	ON	P (%)	53.00	78.80	73.20	64.89	71.95
		R (%)	32.82	51.42	29.46	37.35	44.26
		F (%)	**40.54**	**62.23**	**42.01**	**47.41**	**54.81**
	OFF	P (%)	36.17	71.31	59.03	48.95	56.16
		R (%)	43.76	63.48	35.27	47.35	52.35
		F (%)	**39.60**	**67.17**	**44.16**	**48.13**	**54.19**
Tweet Set-2	ON	P (%)	58.22	58.73	70.67	60.20	67.29
		R (%)	22.87	38.74	12.96	22.13	34.89
		F (%)	**32.84**	**46.69**	**21.90**	**32.36**	**45.95**
	OFF	P (%)	36.80	44.61	32.43	37.61	46.24
		R (%)	43.41	62.83	17.60	38.43	47.64
		F (%)	**39.83**	**52.17**	**22.82**	**38.01**	**46.93**

Table 5: NER Evaluation Results After Diacritics-Based Expansion of Resources (Partial Metrics).

Data Set	Capitalization	Metric	Person	Location	Organization	Overall for PLOs	Overall for 7 Types
Tweet Set-1	ON	P (%)	65.58	87.46	88.76	76.81	81.44
		R (%)	39.38	56.12	33.62	42.80	48.98
		F (%)	**49.21**	**68.37**	**48.77**	**54.97**	**61.17**
	OFF	P (%)	42.21	79.17	69.00	56.02	62.49
		R (%)	51.56	69.85	39.70	53.88	57.90
		F (%)	**46.42**	**74.22**	**50.40**	**54.93**	**60.11**
Tweet Set-2	ON	P (%)	71.48	61.29	72.97	69.07	73.68
		R (%)	26.68	40.21	13.24	24.51	37.47
		F (%)	**38.86**	**48.56**	**22.41**	**36.18**	**49.67**
	OFF	P (%)	42.26	47.07	33.33	41.75	50.23
		R (%)	50.14	66.76	18.04	42.65	51.72
		F (%)	**45.86**	**55.21**	**23.41**	**42.20**	**50.96**

about 6.3% of all NEs in $Tweet\ Set{-}1$ are written in characters with missing diacritics. A plausible alternative to this feature would be to perform diacritics-based correction (or, normalization) as presented in studies like (Mihalcea, 2002) prior to the actual NER procedure. Similar approaches can be tested on tweets in other languages having common characters with diacritics.

3.3 Tweet Normalization

Tweet normalization has emerged as an important research problem (Han and Baldwin, 2011), the solutions to which can readily be used in systems for sentiment analysis and NER (as considered in studies such as (Liu et al., 2012)), among others. In order to observe the effects of normalization on NER performance on Turkish tweets, we have first experimented with a simplistic tweet normalization scheme which aims at decreasing repeated characters in words, as repetition of characters in tweets is a frequent means to express stress. The scheme is outlined below:

1. In order to determine the list of valid Turkish words with consecutively repeated characters, we have employed the list of Turkish unique words (Zemberek, 2010), that we have previously utilized during the diacritics-based resource expansion procedure in Section 3.2.2. Within this list, 74,262 words (about 6.5% of the list) turn out to have consecutively repeated characters.
2. Using this sublist as a reference resource, we have implemented the actual simplistic normalization scheme: if a word in a tweet has consecutively repeated character sequences and the word is not included within the aforementioned sublist, then all of these character sequences are contracted to single character instances. For instance, with this procedure, the token $zamaanlaaa$ is correctly replaced with $zamanla$ (meaning $with\ time$) and $mirayyy$ is correctly replaced with $miray$ (a proper person name).

The employment of the above normalization scheme prior to the actual NER procedure has led to slightly poorer results as some NEs which should not be normalized through this scheme are normalized instead. For instance, the city name *Çanakkale* is changed to *Çanakale* during the normalization procedure and it is missed by the subsequent NER procedure. Hence, we employ a three-phase pipelined NER approach where we first run the NER procedure on the input text, then employ the normalization scheme on the NER output, and finally run the NER procedure again on the normalization output, in order to avoid that the normalization step corrupts well-formed NEs that can readily be extracted by the system.

The performance of this ultimate NER pipeline, with the capitalization feature turned off during both of the actual NER phases, is evaluated only on $Tweet\ Set{-}1$. Therefore, the performance evaluations of the first NER phase correspond to the previously presented results in the rows 4-6 of Table 2 and Table 3, with strict and partial versions of the metrics, respectively.

Below we summarize our findings regarding the intermediate normalization procedure employed, based on its evaluation results. Although some of these findings are not directly relevant for the purposes of the NER procedure, we provide them for the completeness of the discussion on the normalization of Turkish tweets.

- Excluding the normalization cases which involve non-alphabetical characters only (like normalizing >>>>>> to >), those that result in a normalized form with a single alphabetical character (like normalizing `oooooo` to `o`), and those that involve emotion expressions (like normalizing `:DDDDD` to `:D`), the number of resulting instances considered for performance evaluation is 494.

- The number of normalization instances in which an incorrect token is precisely converted into its corresponding valid form is 253, so, the precision of the overall normalization scheme is 51.21%.

- 117 of the incorrect cases are due to the fact that the token that is considered for normalization is a valid but foreign token (such as normalizing $Harry$ to $Hary$, $jennifer$ to $jenifer$, $full$ to ful, and $tweet$ to $twet$). Hence, these cases account for a decrease of 23.68% in the precision of the normalization scheme.

- 15 of the incorrect instances are due to the fact that Turkish characters with diacritics are not correctly used, hence they cannot be found within the reference sublist of valid Turkish words, and subsequently considered by the normalization procedure, although they could instead be subject to a diacritics-based normalization, as pointed out at the end of Section 3.2.2. For instance, *şiir* (meaning $poem$) is incorrectly written as $siir$ in a tweet and since it, in this incorrect form, cannot be found on the reference sublist, it is erroneously changed to sir. There are also other incorrect instances in which superfluous characters are correctly removed with the normalization procedure, yet the resulting token is still not in its correct form as a subsequent diacritics-based correction is required. Though they are not considerably frequent (as we only consider here tokens with consecutively repeated characters), these instances serve to confirm that the restoration of diacritics should be considered along with other forms of normalization.

- Some other frequent errors made by the normalization scheme are due to incorrect tokenization as whitespaces to separate tokens can be missing due to writing errors or the tendency to write some phrases hashtag-like. An example case is incorrectly writing the adverb, $demek\ ki$ (meaning so or $that\ means$), as $demekki$ in a tweet, which in turn is erroneously changed to $demeki$ during normalization. This token, $demekki$, should not be considered within this type of normalization at all, although it needs processing to be transformed into its correct form, $demek\ ki$.

To summarize, the normalization scheme can be enhanced considering the above points, where proper treatment of non-Turkish tokens and the consideration of diacritics-based issues stand as the most promising directions of improvement. Other more elaborate ways of normalizing tweets, as presented in studies such as (Han and Baldwin, 2011), should also be tested together with the NER procedure, to observe their ultimate contribution. Along the way, a normalization dictionary for Turkish can be compiled, following studies like (Han et al., 2012).

The evaluation results of the ultimate three-phase NER pipeline are provided in Table 6, with the systems's capitalization feature turned off in both NER phases. Within the first three rows, the results with the strict evaluation metrics are displayed while the last three rows present those results obtained with the partial versions. When we examine the individual NER results after the incorporation of normalization scheme in details, we observe that there are cases where incorrectly normalizing some common names or slang/contracted words leads to them being extracted as NEs during the second NER phase. In order to prevent such

Table 6: Evaluation Results of the NER Pipeline with Normalization, on $Tweet\ Set{-}1$.

Metric Type	Metric	Person	Location	Organization	Overall for PLOs	Overall for 7 Types
Strict	P (%)	36.45	71.72	58.99	48.94	55.91
	R (%)	44.42	62.06	34.02	46.94	51.20
	F (%)	**40.04**	**66.54**	**43.16**	**47.92**	**53.45**
Partial	P (%)	42.32	78.68	69.35	55.73	62.04
	R (%)	52.07	67.71	38.43	53.18	56.48
	F (%)	**46.69**	**72.78**	**49.45**	**54.43**	**59.13**

false positives, the ways of improving the normalization procedure discussed above can be implemented and thereby less errors will be propagated into the second NER phase.

Though the overall results in Table 6 are slightly better than their counterparts when normalization is not employed, we cannot derive sound conclusions about the contribution of this normalization scheme to the overall NER procedure. The slight improvement is also an expected result as the size of the test data set is quite small and the number of NEs to be recognized after this type of normalization is already limited since only about 1% of all PLOs in $Tweet\ Set{-}1$ have incorrectly repeated consecutive characters. Yet, the results are still promising in that with a more elaborate normalization procedure evaluated on larger corpora, more dramatic increases in the NER performance can be obtained on Turkish tweets.

4 Future Work

Directions of future work based on the current study include the following:

- Following the points made throughout Section 3, several normalization schemes also involving case and diacritics restoration can be implemented and incorporated into the NER procedure on tweets.

- Since tweet texts are short and informal, they often lack contextual clues needed to perform an efficient NER procedure. Additionally, there is a tendency to mention new and popular NEs in tweets which might be missed by a NER system with static lexical resources. Hence, extending the lexical resources of the NER system with contemporary up-to-date NEs automatically obtained from Turkish news articles can be considered. For this purpose, we can readily employ resources like JRC-Names (Steinberger et al., 2011), a publicly available continuously-updated NE and name variant dictionary, as a source of up-to-date NEs in Turkish.

5 Conclusion

In this study, we target the problem of named entity recognition on Turkish tweets. We have carried out experiments starting with a rule-based recognition system and gradually extended it in two directions: adapting the rules/resources of the system and introducing a tweet normalization scheme into the recognition procedure. Thereby, we present our findings on named entity recognition on Turkish tweets in addition to those on the normalization of Turkish tweets. Based on these findings, we outline some desirable features of a named entity recognition system tailored to Turkish tweets. Future work includes the employment and testing of more elaborate tweet normalization procedures along the way, on larger tweet data sets, in addition to evaluating the system after its resources are automatically extended with dictionaries of up-to-date named entities.

Acknowledgments

This study is supported in part by a postdoctoral research grant from TÜBİTAK.

References

Fabian Abel, Qi Gao, Geert-Jan Houben, and Ke Tao. 2011. Analyzing Temporal Dynamics in Twitter Profiles for Personalized Recommendations in the Social Web. In *Proceedings of the 3rd ACM International Web Science Conference*.

Kalina Bontcheva, Leon Derczynski, Adam Funk, Mark Greenwood, Diana Maynard, and Niraj Aswani. 2013. TwitIE: An Open-Source Information Extraction Pipeline for Microblog Text. In *Proceedings of the International Conference on Recent Advances in Natural Language Processing*.

Gökhan Çelikkaya, Dilara Torunoğlu, and Gülşen Eryiğit. 2013. Named Entity Recognition on Real Data: A Preliminary Investigation for Turkish. In *Proceedings of the 7th International Conference on Application of Information and Communication Technologies*.

Gökhan A. Şeker and Gülşen Eryiğit. 2012. Initial Explorations on Using CRFs for Turkish Named

Entity Recognition. In *Proceedings of the International Conference on Computational Linguistics*, pages 2459–2474.

Diego Marinho de Oliveira, Alberto H.F. Laender, Adriano Veloso, and Altigran S. da Silva. 2013. FS-NER: A Lightweight Filter-Stream Approach to Named Entity Recognition on Twitter Data. In *Proceedings of the 22nd International Conference on World Wide Web Companion*, pages 597–604.

Bo Han and Timothy Baldwin. 2011. Lexical Normalisation of Short Text Messages: Makn Sens a #twitter. In *Proceedings of the 49th Annual Meeting of the Association for Computational Linguistics*, pages 368–378.

Bo Han, Paul Cook, and Timothy Baldwin. 2012. Automatically Constructing a Normalisation Dictionary for Microblogs. In *Proceedings of the Joint Conference on Empirical Methods in Natural Language Processing and Computational Natural Language Learning*.

Jason J. Jung. 2012. Online Named Entity Recognition Method for Microtexts in Social Networking Services: A Case Study of Twitter. *Expert Systems with Applications*, 39(9):8066–8070.

Dilek Küçük and Adnan Yazıcı. 2009. Named Entity Recognition Experiments on Turkish Texts. In T. Andreasen et al., editor, *Proceedings of the International Conference on Flexible Query Answering Systems*, volume 5822 of *Lecture Notes in Computer Science*, pages 524–535.

Dilek Küçük and Adnan Yazıcı. 2012. A Hybrid Named Entity Recognizer for Turkish. *Expert Systems with Applications*, 39(3):2733–2742.

Dilek Küçük, Guillaume Jacquet, and Ralf Steinberger. 2014. Named Entity Recognition on Turkish Tweets. In *Proceedings of the Language Resources and Evaluation Conference*.

Chenliang Li, Jianshu Weng, Qi He, Yuxia Yao, Anwitaman Datta, Aixin Sun, and Bu-Sung Lee. 2012. TwiNER: Named Entity Recognition in Targeted Twitter Stream. In *Proceedings of the 35th International ACM SIGIR Conference on Research and Development in Information Retrieval*, pages 721–730.

Xiaohua Liu, Shaodian Zhang, Furu Wei, and Ming Zhou. 2011. Recognizing Named Entities in Tweets. In *Proceedings of the 49th Annual Meeting of the Association for Computational Linguistics: Human Language Technologies - Volume 1*, pages 359–367.

Xiaohua Liu, Ming Zhou, Furu Wei, Zhongyang Fu, and Xiangyang Zhou. 2012. Joint Inference of Named Entity Recognition and Normalization for Tweets. In *Proceedings of the 50th Annual Meeting of the Association for Computational Linguistics: Long Papers - Volume 1*, pages 526–535.

Diana Maynard, Valentin Tablan, Cristan Ursu, Hamish Cunningham, and Yorick Wilks. 2001. Named entity recognition from diverse text types. In *Proceedings of the Conference on Recent Advances in Natural Language Processing*.

Rada F. Mihalcea. 2002. Diacritics Restoration: Learning from Letters versus Learning from Words. In *Proceedings of the 3rd International Conference on Intelligent Text Processing and Computational Linguistics*, pages 339–348.

Jakub Piskorski and Maud Ehrmann. 2013. On Named Entity Recognition in Targeted Twitter Streams in Polish. In *Proceedings of the ACL Workshop on Balto-Slavic Natural Language Processing*.

Bruno Pouliquen and Ralf Steinberger. 2009. Automatic Construction of Multilingual Name Dictionaries. In C. Goutte et al., editor, *Learning Machine Translation*, Advances in Neural Information Processing Systems Series, pages 59–78. MIT Press.

Alan Ritter, Sam Clark, Mausam, and Oren Etzioni. 2011. Named Entity Recognition in Tweets: An Experimental Study. In *Proceedings of the Conference on Empirical Methods in Natural Language Processing*, pages 1524–1534.

Alan Ritter, Mausam, Oren Etzioni, and Sam Clark. 2012. Open Domain Event Extraction from Twitter. In *Proceedings of the 18th ACM SIGKDD International Conference on Knowledge Discovery and Data Mining*, pages 1104–1112.

Bilge Say, Deniz Zeyrek, Kemal Oflazer, and Umut Özge. 2002. Development of a Corpus and a Treebank for Present-Day Written Turkish. In *Proceedings of the 11th International Conference of Turkish Linguistics*.

Ralf Steinberger, Bruno Pouliquen, Mijail Alexandrov Kabadjov, Jenya Belyaeva, and Erik Van der Goot. 2011. JRC-Names: A Freely Available, Highly Multilingual Named Entity Resource. In *Proceedings of the Conference on Recent Advances in Natural Language Processing*.

Serhan Tatar and İlyas Çicekli. 2011. Automatic Rule Learning Exploiting Morphological Features for Named Entity Recognition in Turkish. *Journal of Information Science*, 37(2):137–151.

Gökhan Tür, Dilek Hakkani-Tür, and Kemal Oflazer. 2003. A Statistical Information Extraction System for Turkish. *Natural Language Engineering*, 9(2):181–210.

Reyyan Yeniterzi. 2011. Exploiting Morphology in Turkish Named Entity Recognition System. In *Proceedings of the ACL Student Session*, pages 105–110.

Zemberek. 2010. Turkish Unique Word List of Zemberek NLP Library for Turkic Languages. Available at `http://zemberek.googlecode.com/files/full.txt.tr.tar.gz`.

Author Index